Clark Weber's Rock and Roll Radio The Fun Years: 1955–1975

By Clark Weber

with Neal Samors
Foreword by Neil Sedaka

Chicago's Books Press

Every Great Climb To The Top
Requires Solid Footing, So These Are The Rocks
Upon Which I Built My Career

My wife Joan who believed from the very beginning!

Our daughters
Ann Gail Lesar
Peggy Jean Barthold
Jeanne Wakenight
Janet Bryan

Mother Weber

And finally my Mother-in Law "Mighty Mouth"
The Inventor of "Wide Load Panty Hose"
Who held her breath
When I marched her daughter
Down the aisle!

Edited by Clark Weber, Neal Samors and Jennifer Samors
Produced by Clark Weber and Neal Samors
Designed by Sam Silvio, Silvio Design, Inc.
Printed in Canada by Friesens Corporation

ISBN: 978-0-9797892-1-2 (Softcover)
ISBN: 978-0-9797892-2-9 (Case)

Front Cover:
Clark Weber at WLS-AM Microphone, 1963.

Back Cover:
WLS Radio 890-AM Advertisement, with Clark Weber, 1963

For more information on this book
as well as Neal Samors' other works visit
www.chicagosbooks.com
Email: NSamors@comcast.net

Table of Contents

Acknowledgements

I want to gratefully acknowledge all of the individuals who have contributed to my career in broadcasting, and especially to those who encouraged me to write this book. It is a challenging process to compile not only the story of my own career in radio, but also to select the most interesting and compelling rock and roll radio related tales from my years as a disc jockey and program director. Those stories include ones about the disc jockeys, rock and roll stars, station managers, and record promoters with whom I interacted from the 1950s through the 1980s.

A special thanks to my wife Joan and to Alan Lesar, Reese Rickards, and Charlie Barthold who first suggested this book years ago. Compiling my memories and finding relevant photographs and memorabilia has been challenging, yet I have had a fun time doing it. Thus, I appreciate those who encouraged me to do this book.

There have been many other individuals who supported this effort, including Rob Hummel, R. Scott Childers, Ron Smith, Kipper McGee, Ron Riley, Jim Scully, Jim Stagg, Jim Feely, Mike McCormick, Tommy Edwards, John Gehron, Don Phillips, Lyle Dean, Harvey Wittenberg, Jim Sharp of Sky Audio, and Paul Gallis. In addition, thanks to all of the radio engineers, producers, general managers, program directors, newsmen and women, and sales people without whose help my career on and off the air would never have flourished.

Thanks to the dozens of other people who jogged my rock and roll memories, from time to time, and, last, but certainly not least, Neal Samors, whose expertise as a publisher and support as a friend helped me to put it all together.

Clark Weber

I can remember it like it was yesterday. It was 1959, and I was driving around Brooklyn, NY in my brand new Chevy Impala, with the top down. As I was cruising around the neighborhood, I turned on the radio in hopes that I would hear something that would make me want to turn up the volume and drive around all afternoon. It's funny that I would hear *Oh, Carol*, the new song that Howard Greenfield and I wrote that had just been released. It's a thrill to hear your song on the radio for the first time. I can't really explain what it's like. Tom Hanks beautifully captured this emotion in his film *That Thing You Do*. The irony behind it all, as I switched to the next station, there it was again. I thought it was Déjà vu. But, when I switched the station for a third time, and I heard it again, it was the first time I realized that the power of radio was going to be the key to my success.

After *Oh Carol* I had several more top ten hits, most notably, *Breaking Up is Hard to Do*, my first #1. It would not be until the 1970s' when the radio would catapult me into superstardom again.

Paul Drew was a Program Director for numerous radio stations across the country, who was an admirer of *Bad Blood*. I have always credited a great part of the success of that song, not only to Elton John's historic backing vocal appearance, but to Paul's intuition that this was a song that needed to shock the airwaves. And it did. *Bad Blood* was another chart-topper.

The days of radio as I know it are all gone. The advent of satellite radio is the closest you can get to the golden days of radio, where they actually play entire songs, instead of a few sound bytes, sandwiched in between two commercials and the nonsensical banter of a disc jockey. Thanks to Clark's book, we will be able to keep the history of Rock and Roll radio alive. Cheers! **Neil Sedaka**

Chapter 1
The Birth of Rock and Roll... Your Parents Were to Blame

Mother Weber used to say that the only one who likes change is a wet baby. The concept of change was certainly in the air for radio and the music industry in the mid-1950s, and those two industries didn't like what was coming. That's the bad news. The good news was that they were about to be saved by good old-fashioned sex, or, to be more exact, the reproductive process— that is—the post- World War II baby boom.

In 1945, with the end of the war, 5.1 million American GIs came home, got married, and produced millions of babies—in that order. Now, a lot of today's generation would find that sequence of baby-making to be quite quaint, but it was the accepted order of events in the '40s and '50s.

As things turned out, it led to the beginning of "rock and roll." On average, a musical trend lasts between 12 to 15 years. That is, as generations of children grow into their teenage years they want to claim their own dress styles, music, and trends, and it begins with teenage girls developing a focus on two things: boys and music. And, that is quite predictable. Whether it was the "bobbysoxers" swooning over Frank Sinatra in the '40s, girls in the '50s going nuts for Frankie Avalon and his beach parties, Fabian, Pat Boone, or Ricky Nelson, or the '60s teenage females falling for the Beatles and Frankie Valli and the Four Seasons. The girls, with their active hormones, led the charge, followed by the boys. The prime exception happened with the rise of Elvis Presley, who was favored by the boys first before the girls began to like him and his music.

Fast forward 10 to 15 years...the children of the '40s, '50s and '60s grew up, married, had their own families, and developed different priorities. Their mania for music took a back seat to other more pressing issues like building careers, parenting, and growing family responsibilities. But, as usual, new generations came along and the whole process started all over again. By about 1955, the Perry Comos, Doris Days, Patti Pages, Frankie Laines, and big bands like Ray Anthony were beginning to run out of fans. That generation had grown up. There was a huge void, and record sales began dropping faster than "Miss Paris's panties." Everything was coming down in a hurry and the record industry, and radio, needed an infusion.

Radio and music remained the focal point of entertainment in the 1950s. The disc jockeys in Chicago during those years included Ernie Simon on WGN, Josh Brady and Mel Bellairs on WBBM, Henry Cook and Jim Conway on WMAQ, and, of course, Howard Miller on WIND. In particular, their morning shows did very well in the ratings. But the programs being aired during the rest of the broadcasting day were beginning to unravel. When I interviewed Mel Bellairs recently, we discussed his live morning show on WBBM in the mid-'50s from 7 A.M. to 9 A.M. every morning. The show was called *The Music Wagon* and it included a live 12-piece orchestra and singers, and the program was making a lot of money. But, the rest of the radio day consisted of 15-minute blocks of programs, including soap operas like *Ma Perkins* and *Backstage Wife* that were network station programs. The independently owned radio stations included live shows like the one done by "Two-Ton Baker, the Music Maker" who did 15 minutes of piano music sponsored by Riverview Park. That was followed by 15 minutes of recorded Freddie Martin music sponsored by Cook County Mobile Homes. That was the way the daytime portions of radio broadcasting existed in those years.

Meanwhile, by 1955, television was coming on like a "runaway freight train." The big sponsors like Ford, Chevrolet, and the cigarette and beer sponsors provided the big advertising dollars and that was primarily being spent on television. While television was taking away most of the national advertising money, radio stations soon recognized that they were in deep trouble because they could not survive on local advertising dollars alone. They needed to have national advertising money: it was true then, it's true today.

What finally drove radio stations from New York to Chicago to Los Angeles to consider a rock and roll format was the fact that both revenue and listening audiences continued in decline. In 1956, a Detroit radio station, WJBK, decided that the future was with the kids, and

"What finally drove radio stations from New York to Chicago to Los Angeles to consider a rock and roll format was the fact that both revenue and listening audiences continued to decline."

the station decided to "bite the bullet." They started rocking with a DJ named Ed McKinzie, who had the show business name of "Jack the Bellboy." McKinzie had a great time when he was on the air, while playing the music the kids wanted to hear. As a result, the show took off, and it wasn't long before WXYZ and other Detroit radio stations followed suit.

However, what really convinced stations to join the rock music revolution was a little "white lie" that ABC television began spreading around the country. It all started in the mid 1950s when that network had the youngest audience and programming. Today, that would be a bonanza, but, in the mid-'50s, it was considered anathema to advertisers. ABC couldn't sell the young demographics that centered around the teenage audience because advertising agencies wouldn't touch that age group. They said it was because there was marketing information to show that the kids didn't have the dollars to justify advertising to them. So, they determined that it was a waste of money. In reaction, ABC began a "full-court press" to convince the ad agencies and sponsors that kids were the coming marketing "messiahs." The network conducted study after study that showed how large the teen market was and how much bigger it was going to be in the near future. Both of those statements were true because of the war babies and the Baby Boomers.

The real "truth stretcher," however, was the projected amount of money the kids were expected to have available for their discretionary spending. While I was an emcee at hundreds of record hops across the Midwest in the '50s and '60s, I observed that most teenagers barely could afford the $.75 admission fee to the dance, much less discretionary income that would be of particular interest to advertisers. ABC countered with the argument: "Yes, maybe they don't have a lot of money now, but someday they'll grow up and have much more money to spend." Then, and now, more money is wasted on bad marketing than any other human activity outside of government expenditures.

Advertisers like Pan Am, TWA, and Braniff Airlines believed that argument about future funds available to teenagers, and those companies decided to spend large amounts of money to reach my WLS teen audience. I would sit there in the morning and wonder why such companies were advertising on my show. And, I don't have to emphasize the fact that all three of those airlines are no longer in business. Of course, the same is true for such former Chicago advertisers as Morris B. Sachs, Robert Hall Clothes, Karroll's Red Hanger Shops, and William A. Lewis: Where the Models Buy Their Clothes.

Chicago radio stations knew they faced a series of major challenges that included the rapid growth in the popularity of television, a dramatic loss of their sponsors, and kids going into movie theaters, jumping up and down and packing the movie houses to see movies like *Blackboard Jungle*. All of a sudden the new singing sensations Bill Haley and the Comets were being heard everywhere with their hit song, *Rock Around the Clock*. At the same time, Elvis's records were flying off the shelves. But the dilemma then was the same one that radio stations face today: if radio stations played those rock and roll songs they would blow out their core audience—people over the age of 25 or 30 who wouldn't listen to that music and would just listen to other stations because the new rock and roll music was so alien to them. It was a discordant sound that adults really didn't like. So, radio stations had to decide if it was worth the risk of losing their traditional audiences and advertising dollars in order to attract the younger kids. For a while, most of the big Chicago radio stations decided to stay the course and refrain from playing rock and roll.

Another developing trend happened when the record companies began to notice that white kids were developing an interest in rhythm and blues music. However, the companies determined that a lot of those same white kids probably wouldn't buy records performed by black artists. So, they began taking some of the very popular R & B songs and re-recording them with white artists. LaVerne Baker was the first one who recorded *Tweedle Dee,* but like a lot of other white disc jockeys, I was playing Georgia Gibbs' version of Baker's song. It was the same thing with the Crewcuts and *Shaboom.* The original version had been recorded by an African American group called The Chords. Bill Haley and the Comets sold millions of dollars worth of *Shake, Rattle and Roll,* while the song had originally been recorded by a black artist named Crazy Joe Turner.

Originally, R&B wasn't even identified as "rock" music. Instead, it was referred to as "race music." Later, it was called "rhythm and blues" because it had been first played by African American musicians who were steeped in the blues that had developed in the South. There were artists like "Butterball" King (later known as B.B. King) one of the early blues singers, Howling Wolf, and Little Richard. All of them had their early start in music playing the blues. The black radio stations played the blues and while Chicago's South Side of town was rocking, on the other sides of town the white radio stations kept their distance. There was just no crossover, and white stations stayed away from that music because they recognized that racism was still a major issue. Even into the '60s, there were some records that weren't played on white stations because the feeling was that they wouldn't be accepted by white audiences.

In the early '50s, Chicago had several black DJs like Jack L. Cooper, Al Benson, Bill Hill, Richard Spam, Sid McCoy, Frank McCarthy, and Lucky Cordell who were having a "rocking good time." When I interviewed Lucky, he said that he and the other black DJs would buy advertising time out of the their own pockets on the South Side radio stations, such as WGES-1390 AM, and then resell the time to sponsors. Cordell said that they made a lot of money selling advertising, and that way, they could play any music they wanted. The stations didn't care about the source of the money and just told the DJs to use the advertising time any way they saw fit. The DJs were able to pick the music they felt would have the greatest appeal to their own listening audiences and then play those records. Lucky also told me that they were doing record hops back in those days in bowling alleys and dance halls in the black neighborhoods. He said that they had a clear sense from their audiences what was popular and what wasn't. Their approach was very successful even to the extent that Al Benson had a television show on the old WBKB-TV (now WLS-TV) that predated *Soul Train* by many, many years and was very popular.

Two Chicago record promoters, Leonard and Phil Chess, who had their studios on South Michigan Avenue, had been recording blues artists for years. Those old friends of mine started to "smell" money and they were right on! While they didn't see rock and roll coming, they had a sense that there was a big market for the blues. They would even take an old tape recorder, hook it up to their auto's battery, and record the blues performers out of the back of their cars. Leonard and Phil slowly began to recognize a growing interest in the white community for rhythm and blues and they started to record just about everybody they could find. As a result, the Chess brothers were making serious money in those years recording rhythm and blues on two different labels. Chess focused on recording rhythm and blues while Checker was recording other artists.

left to right
**Bob "Coffee Head" Larsen,
Lee Rothman, Clark Weber,
Sam Holman, Don Phillips.
The man holding the phone
is singer and band leader,
Vaughn Monroe.**

"In the '50s and '60s, it didn't take too much to have the Federal Communications Commission (FCC) come "knocking on your door."

Although the rhythm and blues lyrics were beginning to be noticed, the songs did include words that raised eyebrows because of their suggestive nature. I guess some things in music never change! In those days, the lyrics were known in the business as "crotch music" and they were not much different from today. It seemed that many of the artists were quite "earthy" in songs like *Short Fat Fanny, Work With Me Annie, I'm A Sixty-Minute Man,* and *My Ding A Ling,* to name a few. R&B was causing problems because many parents were upset by some of those song titles and lyrics, and they were putting pressure on some of the radio stations not to play those songs. As a result, radio stations were concerned about losing their FCC licenses.

In the '50s and '60s, it didn't take too much to have the Federal Communications Commission (FCC) come "knocking on your door." Although the FCC today is somewhat of a "paper tiger," back then when the FCC contacted a station or visited in person, stations tended to respond quickly, and as a result they walked a very fine line. Radio stations in those years were so well regulatedthat if one of the tower lights on a station's antenna burned out, they were required, by law, to immediately send a telegram to the FCC in Washington, D.C. It meant that they had to quickly fix the tower light, and the FCC would also send out a notice to pilots telling them of the potential danger to navigation. A station actually had 24 hours for somebody to climb up their tower and replace the bulb. In those years, stations had to cross every "t" and dot every "i." Otherwise, you would incur FCC wrath.

One major event in rock and roll radio happened in the mid-'50s when a hard-driving, hard-drinking, white DJ in Cleveland named Alan "Moon Doggie" Freed started reaching out to his young listeners at 10:00 P.M. on Cincinnati's WLW. At that time of night, you couldn't give the advertising away, much the same as it is today. Freed went to WLW and said that he could put on a show for the kids, and the station's response was, "Okay, go ahead because at 10:00 P.M. it probably can't hurt!" Freed simply had a strong sense of the potential positive response by the kids to rock and roll, as well as rhythm and blues, and he began playing that music at night. In response, the kids just went absolutely crazy. Like WLS-AM in Chicago in the '60s, WLW was a 50,000 watt clear channel station that was able to reach out at night to kids across the country, and Freed and his "Moon Doggie" persona was greeted with open arms by teenagers looking to find their own particular kind of music. Young listeners began flocking to Freed's show, and it wasn't long before other "white stations" noticed his success. Simply put: the "cork was out of the bottle." Even WGN-AM in Chicago was attracted to WLW's new found success.

Freed quickly realized the overwhelmingly positive response to the music he was playing and decided to put on live shows at theaters in Philadelphia, Cleveland, Boston, and New York, and the kids went nuts. His show included live acts like Fats Domino, Rufus Thomas, and Lloyd Price, early rhythm and blues singers who had morphed into rock and roll stars in the late '50s. As a result, Freed made a lot of money on his stage show. In fact, in some of those towns, he was even arrested and that fueled the fire. As a result of Freed's successes, he was hired by CBS-TV to create a program called *Rock and Roll Dance Party*. It was there, in 1955, that Freed came face-to-face with the race issue, something which he apparently didn't see coming.

In fact, the whole event was spontaneous. One of the artists on Freed's show, a kid named Frankie Lymon along with his group called The Teenagers, were performing their hit song, *Why Do Fools Fall In Love?"* Lymon, who was an African American, got caught up in the enthusiasm, stepped off the bandstand into the audience and began dancing with a white girl. Wow, did that create an explosion, and the event caused such an outcry from some white

left to right
"Coffee Head" Larsen, Lee Rothman, Bob Kelly, Woody Welch, and Clark Weber.

COFFEE HEAD LARSEN

LEE ROTHMAN

Wonderful

W

24 HOU

BOB KELLY   WOODY WELCH   CLARK WEBER

RIT

RS EVERY DAY 1340

parents that CBS was forced to cancel Freed's show. I met Frankie and thought he was a nice guy, but, tragically, he died at a young age.

Peter Potter hosted a show on the West Coast that was similar to Freed's. It was called *Juke Box Jury*, and about the time that CBS cancelled Freed's show, Potter spoke out and was reported to have expressed a view that slammed rock music by saying that, "All rhythm and blues records are dirty and as bad for kids as dope." Two things happened: a lot of parents joined in the protest and said "Yeah, right on", while many kids responded with, "Oh, no. This is our music." At about that same time, the churches were becoming aware of rock and roll and the songs' lyrics. In Chicago, the Catholic Archdiocese and Cardinal Stritch decided to ban rock and roll from being played or performed at any Catholic school events. They determined that such music was hedonistic and based on tribal rhythms, and, of course, that made the Chicago radio stations nervous.

In April 1955, Catholic high schools in Chicago, probably at the urging of the Archdiocese, got together and flooded WIND and WJJD, two of Chicago's most popular radio stations, with over 15,000 letters complaining about rock and roll music. And the stations really paid attention to the protest because the heat was intense. Ironically, only a couple of years later, the local Catholic Youth Organizations (CYOs) sponsored weekly sock-hops in the Chicago area. I emceed many of those sock-hops, and they brought in a ton of cash money for the Catholic Church. So, they eventually began to realize that there was money to be made from playing rock and roll at their events, and got on board.

About that time, the very popular television show, *Your Lucky Strike Hit Parade*, starring Snookie Lanson and other singers, began to lose ratings and the show was eventually cancelled. It was simply because the *Hit Parade* singers like Snookie Lanson and Giselle McKenzie couldn't imitate the rock singers who were beginning to perform their own songs on television. The kids wanted to hear the actual rock and roll performers, and such programs as Dick Clark's *American Bandstand* grew rapidly in popularity. The cancellation of *Your Hit Parade* signified the end of an era in music and television, and although the change in teenagers' tastes in music upset a lot of adults, especially parents of teenagers, the parents were not really prepared for the shift in tastes.

One other thing that helped tip the scales in favor of rock and roll was the introduction of 45 rpm records. Although they had been available since 1949, radio stations hesitated to play them because it required the purchase of new turntables. At that time, the stations were playing songs on 78 and 33 1/3 rpm records. When RCA began manufacturing the 45 rpm record changers in the mid-'50s, 13 million teenagers went crazy, and since the new records were selling for around $.89 each, the kids bought 75 million of them in a very short period of time. Reluctantly, the radio stations finally began buying turntables that could play 45 rpm records.

There is one common thread in the history of Chicago's rock radio and disc jockeys that was shared by almost every one of those deejays, including me. We loved what we were doing for a living, and it showed. You could tell because there was an excitement that came through the microphones which teenagers could easily identify. There were DJs like Dick Biondi on WLS-AM who were reaching out to the teenagers like "pied pipers," and listeners could hear that on their radios. Others, like my "arch-nemesis" on WLS, Ron Riley, had an animal magnetism about him.

There were various disc jockeys working in Chicago in those years that only lasted a few months or a year or two at the various stations. Then, there were others who remained on the air for years until their listening audiences actually grew tired of them, or the DJs grew tired of the music. However, I think that all of them would agree that it was a wonderful ride while it lasted. Among those who only lasted a few months, some just didn't like the work, while, in other instances it was their wives who didn't like Chicago and wanted to move away. In one case, there was one deejay who worked the all-night show on WLS. However, because he was a diabetic, he couldn't get his insulin adjusted while working those strenuous hours. In fact, he went into a diabetic coma three different times while on the all-night show. As a result, he came to Gene Taylor, the station's program director, and said that he couldn't adapt, and because he had a young family he decided to leave the station. Another deejay's wife didn't like Chicago, and they moved back to Louisville after a short time.

There were a few DJs who did come away with fame and riches. There were also some who wound up dead broke with nothing but a scrapbook full of memories. Of course, alcohol and drugs wiped out some good friends of mine. And, there were more than a few who after they had been disc jockeys walked away from the jobs, saying, "I've had enough and I want to go on from here." There was also more than a parallel between some disc jockeys and the "one-hit wonder" pop singers. Ironically, there were more than a few disc jockeys who really made it big in Chicago and then walked away from it: Ron Riley and Bob Hale; Brent Miller and Bob Sirott who went into television; Bob Del Giorno from WIND opened up several successful restaurants in California, and he is still running them; Connie Szerszen, also from WIND, became a portrait painter; and, others like Howard Miller, Bob Dearborn, and Dex Card who became successful radio station owners. Now, the one common thread for each was that they had a wonderful gift called "choice." It's such a simple word, yet a lot of people have a difficult time accepting it. To a great degree we decide our own lives...rich, poor, fat, thin, bashful, or bold. Each one of us, disc jockeys included, make choices both good and bad every day. Or, we'll blame others for the bad decisions in our lives! A lot of people find excuses and say, "Well, I was born fat...or, I was never good at math." We all make choices but there are others who just don't want to choose because they might fail, or worse yet, they might succeed.

A couple of months ago, I gave a talk to a group of communications students at Columbia College on the subject of careers in broadcasting. One of the questions was, "What happens if I choose radio and fail?" Well, my answer was, "Of course you're going to fail!" And, the faces around the room fell. These college students looked at me like I had just destroyed their career. Then, I explained to them that was how we learned and that all success was built on a foundation of failure. There is no failure in falling down...failure is in not getting up. Now, you can believe that or not, but, again, that's your choice!

Chapter 2
"I Didn't Get the Girl, But I Did Get the Career"

There is a fine line between a hobby and insanity, and I think that I crossed that line several times in my lifetime. Combined with the discovery from a young age that I was blessed with the ability to entertain people, I was left with the need to make some serious career choices.

Three events took place when I was young that led to an eventual career in radio. The first happened in 1941, when I was 10 years old. I learned that my Uncle Alex had a hobby as an amateur radio operator, or "ham." His call letters were W9KHE, and I would sit at his side while he talked to the world via shortwave radio. To this day I can't exactly explain how or why it happened, but I was absolutely thrilled at the sights and sounds of ham radio. It was probably the combination of the eerie blue glow of mercury vapor emanating from the radio's mercury tubes and hearing a cacophony of voices from across the globe that blew me away. Even Morse Code, which I couldn't understand at the time, had a magic sound to it. But, as a result of the outbreak of World War II, the FCC closed down amateur radio for the duration of the war.

The second event happened to me a few years later while I was in eighth grade. I went to the movies and saw a film starring the young, and then unknown comedian, Sid Caesar. He did a standup routine in which he played a WWII fighter pilot named "Smiling Jim," complete with vocal sound effects. In that role he pretended to fight off enemy planes against great odds, all the while smiling. I sat through the movie twice in order to watch the routine, and I came away thinking, "I can do that!" I practiced it and, a few weeks later, at a party with other teenagers, I performed Caesar's routine. Before I knew it, I was being invited to other parties and soon became a center of attention. As an eighth grader, that's pretty heady stuff! Then, I was selected to play the lead role in our eighth grade graduation play, *Elmer*, and with my few funny lines and the response to them, I realized that I had a desire to entertain.

Letter addressed to Clarence Weber, "aka Clark"

The third event happened during junior high school when my English teacher commented to me that I seemed very comfortable speaking in front of her class. Years later, I told that teacher, Miss Manning, how important her seemingly innocuous remark was in helping propel my future career. Then, at Wauwatosa High School, it was more of the same since with little effort I could hold the attention of my speech class and entertain the students with ease.

The war ended in 1945, and amateur radio operators were once again allowed to broadcast over the airways. I jumped into the hobby with both feet, and when I was 16 years old I received my ham radio license, as W9FFB, and began talking to the world via shortwave. Today I might be classified as a geek or a tech head, but my fellow teenaged ham operators and I lived and breathed the hobby 24 hours a day.

Now, there has to be a girl in every story and, in my case, there was one special female who became the focus of my imaginary affection. During my junior year at Wauwatosa High School, I began to notice a young lady in my homeroom named Barbara Taylor. It was strictly worship from afar because I never summoned up the nerve to ask her out on a date. You talk about shy! We would occasionally talk in front of our lockers and all the while I was thinking that she was the neatest girl in my class. I wanted to impress her but didn't know how to accomplish that daunting feat. However, one day, I saw an article in the school newspaper that I thought would knock her socks off. A local radio station in Milwaukee, WFOX, invited high school students to apply to be a guest DJ at their station, with the opportunity to introduce one record. I thought to myself, "What a great way to impress Barbara Taylor!"

I fired off a letter to the radio station, and, to my amazement I received an invitation from WFOX to be on the air on March 18, 1948. I proudly told Barbara about my upcoming appearance and asked her to be sure to listen to me on the program. When I walked into the radio station I never felt so comfortable in my life. To this day, I cannot explain that wonderful feeling and the fact that I thought I was fearless and just filled with wide-eyed interest. The WFOX DJ talked to me for a few minutes, and then he allowed me to dedicate

March 4, 1948

Mr. ClarenceWeber
718 N. 115th Street
Milwaukee 13, Wisconsin

Dear Clarence:

I have made arrangements for you to be guest
disc jocky on "It's Hi Time" on Wednesday,
March 10, between 7:30 and 7:45 a.m.

Please arrive at the studios around 7 a.m.
so that you can pick out some of the records
you would like to hear.

Our studios are at 739 North Broadway in downtown Milwaukee. If the elevators are not in
operation when you arrive, take the stairs to
the third floor and turn to the right.

See you on the 10th!

Sincerely,

Ken Hegard

"There has to be a girl in every story and, in my case, there was one special female who became the focus of my imaginary affection.

Clark Weber in 1957 while standing in front of a microphone with the call letters, WBKV, West Bend, Wisconsin.

"I couldn't have had a more understanding wife in the world, and if your mate understands and accepts all of the ups and downs of a radio career, you are halfway to success."

a popular song called *The Sabre Dance* to Barbara. However, in only 15 minutes, my appearance was finished. As I left the station, I had an epiphany and knew what I wanted to do for the rest of my life. It was as simple as that: I wanted a career in radio.

From that day forward, even though I was only 17 years old, I told everyone I knew that I had found my true calling in life. The only negative part of the story was that Barbara forgot to listen to me on the program that morning and missed my big moment. Ironically, years later, at a high school reunion, I told her the story but her reaction surprised me. She said, "I didn't even know you liked me." So, for me, it ended up being just a teenage infatuation with no measurable romantic outcome.

In 1950, I went to college at the University of Wisconsin-Milwaukee, but since the school's Speech Department didn't offer any program that would prepare me for a career in radio, I choose business as my major. That was the first of two dumb moves that I made as an 18-year-old. The other one involved joining the U.S. Naval Reserve although it eventually meant operating Navy radios and putting on a sailor suit. It cost me dearly. Less than one year at UWM, in August 1950, the Korean War broke out and you can guess who was called to active duty. The Navy was kind enough to point out that if I selected the regular Navy, in return for a commitment of four years in service, I would receive free schooling in and out of the service. I signed up and spent three years, 11 months, and 16 days serving in the Navy. But, who was counting!

I ended up seeing combat in Korea as a radio operator, while in an amphibious unit aboard the USS LSMR 527, shooting rockets at the North Korean Army. Also, while in the Navy, I began taking private flying lessons and was badly smitten by that bug. I have continued a personal love affair with the sky and airplanes, later owning several airplanes, and I can only describe flying as a thrill I have never tired of.

During those years in the Navy, I couldn't wait for the time to pass so that I could get back to civilian status. Once home, I had a couple of decisions to make: choose to return to college, which would be paid for by Uncle Sam; or, begin knocking on radio station doors in order to find a job in broadcasting. One would think that would be a no-brainer, but it wasn't! About that same time, my social life took a fortuitous turn when my cousin fixed me up on a blind date. The young lady, Joan Brouillette, was a student nurse at Milwaukee County Hospital. She was bright, charming, and it didn't hurt that she was also quite good looking. Joan and I didn't hit it off on the first date, or the second, for that matter. There almost wasn't a third date, but I had two things going for me: I was polite and persistent. By the fourth date, she began to find some redeeming qualities in me and soon we were going steady.

I decided to forego completing my college degree and strike out for a career in radio. That decision did not come easily since Joan was graduating from college and had accomplished her goal of a medical education in nursing. After several long talks, Joan lovingly said that she would support me in whatever decision I made about a career. Ironically, today when I am asked by young people whether they should finish college, I tell them that if they aspire to go into broadcasting they should first complete their degree. The odds of making a long and healthy career in radio are about as risky as defusing roadside bombs in Iraq. Simply put, everyone needs to have a fallback position and an education can give you that protection.

Within months of my decision to pursue a broadcasting career, I was hired by WAUX in Waukesha, Wisconsin. I thought that I had died and gone to heaven even though the hours were long and the pay was pitiful since I began at a salary of $60 a week. But, I figured it was worth it since I was on my way as a radio broadcaster. A year later, WBKV in West Bend, Wisconsin wooed me away with a $15 a week raise. The station played mostly polka music, but they also did a "Man on the Street" interview show each day from Main Street in downtown West Bend. I was just awful in that role, but since I co-hosted the show with Ray Kessenich, a fellow announcer who fortunately knew what he was doing, it all worked out. I carefully observed him and learned the new skill of interviewing people that would help me years later as a talk show host.

My radio shift at WBKV was noon to signoff, which during the summer months was 7:00 P.M. in the evening. Darn few polka fans were listening late in the day, so I took a chance and on Saturday evenings I began sneaking in a bit of rock and roll. I had to pay for those records out of my own pocket, and the first one I bought was by Gene Vincent and the Blue Caps called *BeBop-A-Lula.* The rock and roll hook was set, and I knew I wanted to reach that audience.

My radio show came to the attention of a Chicago record promoter named Paul Gallis. He told me that a Milwaukee rock station, WRIT, was looking for an all-night DJ and that I should apply for the job. Although I had just two and a half years of experience under my belt, I was hired by WRIT at $125 a week to do their all-night show. Meanwhile, by that time, Joan and I had married and had our first two children: Ann, our 2-year-old daughter; and, Peggy, our one-year-old. Apparently there was too much "rocking" at home because, within another year, we had twin daughters named Jeanne and Janet. So, we were the parents of four girls who had been born within 27 months of each other—Joan said that she was beginning to run out of names to call me!

When my wife and I would talk about my future goal in radio, Chicago was always the focus of discussion. That was the radio market where I wanted to be, but I didn't have the least idea how to get hired by a station in "the Toddlin Town." Although I wasn't bright enough to lay the groundwork for it to happen, fate stepped in.

Within two years of working in Milwaukee, I was doing the morning show at WRIT. The guy who was the mid-morning DJ was a man named Sam Holman. Sam was an easy going, fun-loving kind of disc jockey who was quite familiar with his radio craft, and did enjoy his alcohol. The only problem was that when Sam drank, he could sometimes become angry. One night, at an RCA promotional party, Sam drank too much and, afterward, as we headed for the parking lot to get my car to drive home, Holman made a disparaging remark to the parking lot attendant. As I recall it, the attendant responded by picking up a tire iron and began swinging it at Holman. His clear intention was to knock Sam silly, but, luckily, I saw a Milwaukee police car coming down the street. I whistled for their attention, they broke up the fight, and Sam, probably under the influence of alcohol, said to me, "Clark, you saved my life, and some day I'll repay the favor!"

Another attendee at that party was Ron Riley who was a DJ from our competition, WOKY. He had also imbibed too much at the party, and the next day, in a kidding way, I took a cheap shot at him on the air. I had the temerity to suggest that Riley might have been drinking too much at the party. I made a joke on the air where I kidded Ron about his behavior at the party. My attempt at humor only helped to set the stage for an ongoing, on-air repartee, and staged "feud" with Riley that continued for years both in Milwaukee, and when we both were hired by WLS in Chicago.

A few months later, Sam left WRIT and went to KQV in Pittsburgh, and that was the last I heard of him until August 1961. He had moved up the corporate ladder of ABC to become program director at WLS-AM in Chicago. WLS had become a roaring success as a rock station soon after switching their format to rock and roll in 1960. Everybody in the radio business was in awe of the station's power and success and WLS was, without a doubt, the "King Kong" of rock and roll radio.

One morning, the phone rang in my office in Milwaukee and, to my surprise, it was Sam. "Remember when you saved my life?" Sam asked. We laughed and I said, "Oh, yeah. You mean I have to save you again?" "No," he said, "it's time to pay you back. How would you like to be my all-night man at WLS on a program we are calling 'East of Midnight?' Come down to Chicago tomorrow and let's talk." I burned rubber all the way down I-94, said yes to the job offer, and then raced back to Milwaukee to share the incredible good news with Joan. My salary suddenly increased from $300 a week in Milwaukee to $650 a week at WLS, plus the opportunity to do many record hops. As far as I was concerned, I was going to be paid a gold mine!

The only flaw in the perfect offer was the fact that Joan and I had purchased a new home in Milwaukee a year earlier, and because of the soft real estate market at that time it would be difficult to sell the house. In fact, it took almost two more years to sell the property. It meant that for the next 18 months, I had a daily commute between Milwaukee and Chicago in order to be the DJ on WLS' all-night show from midnight to 5:00 A.M. It damned near killed me since it was a three-hour commute each way. The situation was also incredibly rough on Joan because I was almost never home, and, for all intents and purposes, she was raising four little girls on her own. I couldn't have had a more understanding wife in the world, and if your mate understands and accepts all of the ups and downs of a radio career, you are halfway to success. If they can't or won't deal with the instability of broadcasting, you should get a job at the post office in order to save your marriage!

Chapter 3
Behind the Scenes–The Fifties Rock and Roll Stars; Early Chicago Rock and Roll Radio Stations: WIND and WJJD

In Chicago, the first two radio stations that began playing rock and roll music early on were WIND (560 AM) and WJJD (1160 AM). WIND was owned by the Westinghouse Broadcasting Company and, beginning in 1947, Howard Miller, their morning man, was consistently among the top money producers for the station. He had a huge following, and his ratings indicated that he was in the lead in the morning, with WGN and WBBM close behind.

"There are several reasons why Chicago couldn't get enough of Howard Miller. He had a law degree and was able to mix his music, conversations, and politics in a way that many people, particularly women, enjoyed."

Miller became so popular that after finishing his morning show on WIND each day, he would leave the Wrigley Building, cross Michigan Avenue, and do a 30-minute record show on WBBM. Later, he also did a one-hour afternoon show on WMAQ. To allow a personality to work under contract for another radio station in that same market was unheard of, and yet, Miller was so popular that WIND was willing to share its star.

There are several reasons why Chicago couldn't get enough of Howard Miller. He had a law degree and was able to mix his music, conversations, and politics in a way that many people, particularly women, enjoyed. He had a huge following among the ladies. Those were the days of women's hose or stockings that were kept up with a garter belt, and each morning Howard would announce, "All right girls, time to roll 'em up and hook 'em!" That was considered pretty racy for the 1950s. His commercial load was so heavy on WIND that Westinghouse had a staff announcer reading many of the live commercials on his show. One of the announcers was an excellent WIND DJ who later became a Hall of Fame play-by-play baseball announcer for both the Cubs and White Sox: Milo Hamilton. Milo recalls reading the live spots on Howard's show for Elam's Ground Cornmeal, Magikist Carpet Cleaner (at Mohawk 4-4100), and Lytton's. Then, later in the day, Milo was a DJ on the air from 5 P.M. to 7 P.M. playing music on his own WIND program.

When WIND began to really rock from 1956 through 1960, the kids flocked to the station and to its record hops. At the time, the Club Boston, at 26th and California, had WIND Sunday record hops with an admission price of $.75. Howard Miller would also pack the Chicago Theatre with live rock groups like Little Richard and the Flamingos, and Milo was introducing singers like Jackie DeShannon and Connie Francis in person at Niles' Maine Township High School on Dempster Street, complete with the live Ted Osling Band. During the summer, even Riverview Park got into the rock and roll action with record hops on weekends. Between riding on the Bobs and the Silver Streak, you could "rock the night away!"

Two other DJs rounded out the WIND staff in the '50s: Dom Quinn and John Doremus. Both of those guys were peerless disc jockeys, and, as well, the other WIND air staff was first rate. Bernie Allen started at the station in 1948 and recalls that the music clock (record schedule) at that time was as follows: 10 minutes, at the top of the hour, for Perry Como; 15 minutes of Freddy Martin; 30 minutes of new hits; 10 minutes of Xavier Cugat and his Latin band; and, finally, 15 minutes of Bing Crosby.

However, what WIND didn't have on the air, and would ultimately cost them the rock and roll crown, was a teenaged "pied piper." They needed someone who was a bit of a rebel and a teen focal point for their music. In short, they needed a Dick Biondi. He was not long in coming to Chicago, but not to WIND. It is interesting to note that in the mid-50s, there were less than a dozen radio stations vying for the Chicago audience, while today there are an estimated 52 stations.

Throughout the 1950s and up to the mid-1960s, Howard Miller was still riding high in the ratings. Then one morning he made some negative comments about the idea of African American men being hired by the Chicago Fire Department. Years later he told me he did it to stir up the audience, and it backfired. As a result of his comments, some members of the city's black community began picketing at WIND, marching back and forth on Michigan Avenue demanding that Miller be fired. That is exactly what the station's general manager did. While the move did serve to placate the angry mob, it sank the station's ratings. With Miller gone, his listening audience soon abandoned WIND en masse and appeared to change their affiliation to WGN. Prior to Miller's firing, WIND, WGN, and my morning show on WLS were

"There were deejays like Dick Biondi on WLS-AM who were reaching out to the teenagers like "pied pipers," and listeners could hear that on their radios."

RADIO CHICAGO
WJJD
A Broadcast Service of Plough, Inc.
1160 On Your Radio Dial

Forty Top Tunes
of Greater Chicago

Top Tunes of Greater Chicago according to Record and Sheet Music Sales, Coin Machine Operators and Radio Requests, as determined by the WJJD Weekly Survey

WJJD FORTY TOP TUNES OF GREATER CHICAGO - WEEK OF OCT. 13, 1958 - SURVEY #19 - VOL. 3

THIS WEEK	TITLE	ARTIST	RECORD NO.	LAST WEEK	WEEKS ON CHART
1.	TOPSY PART TWO	COZY COLE	LOVE 5004	5	3
2.	IT'S ALL IN THE GAME	TOMMY EDWARDS	MGM 12688	1	11
3.	CHANTILLY LACE	BIG BOPPER	MER 71343	2	7
4.	TEA FOR TWO CHA CHA	TOMMY DORSEY	DEC 30704	3	6
5.	VOLARE (NEL BLU DI PINTO DI BLU)	DOMENICO MODUGNO	DEC 30677	4	13
6.	TO KNOW HIM IS TO LOVE HIM	TEDDY BEARS	DORE 503	20	2
7.	LEAVE ME ALONE	DICKY DOO & DONTS	SWAN 4014	10	4
8.	DEVOTED TO YOU	EVERLY BROTHERS	CAD 1350	7	11
9.	SUSIE DARLIN'	ROBIN LUKE	DOT 15781	6	8
10.	DAY THE RAINS CAME	JANE MORGAN	KAPP 253	16	3
10a.	DAY THE RAINS CAME	RAYMOND LEFEVRE	KAPP 231	16a	3
11.	IT'S ONLY MAKE BELIEVE	CONWAY TWITTY	MGM 12677	24	3
12.	HULA HOOP	TERESA BREWER	COR 62003	13	4
12a.	HULA HOOP	GEORGIA GIBBS	ROU 4016	13a	4
13.	TEARS ON MY PILLOW	IMPERIALS	END 1027	8	9
14.	NEAR YOU	ROGER WILLIAMS	KAPP 233	9	9
15.	WHO ARE THEY TO SAY	DECASTRO SISTERS	ABC 9932	11	7
16.	FIREFLY	TONY BENNETT	COL 41237	21	3
17.	SUMMERTIME BLUES	EDDIE COCHRAN	LIB 55144	12	6
18.	QUEEN OF THE HOP	BOBBY DARIN	ATCO 6127	32	2
19.	NINE MORE MILES	GEORGE YOUNG	CAMEO 150	14	5
20.	NO ONE BUT YOU	AMES BROS.	RCA 7315	27	3
21.	JUST YOUNG	PAUL ANKA	ABC 9956	28	4
22.	YOU CHEATED	SHIELDS	DOT 15805	22	6
22a.	YOU CHEATED	DEL VIKINGS	MER 71345	22a	6
23.	MY LUCKY LOVE	DOUG FRANKLIN	COLONIAL 7777	19	6
24.	TOM DOOLEY	KINGSTON TRIO	CAP 4049	--	1
25.	ARE YOU REALLY MINE	JIMMY RODGERS	ROU 4090	18	10
26.	CALL ME	JOHNNY MATHIS	COL 41253	37	2
27.	MEXICAN HAT ROCK	APPLE JACKS	CAMEO 149	29	3
28.	FIBBIN'	PATTI PAGE	MER 71355	31	5
29.	NO ONE KNOWS	DION & BELMONTS	LAURIE 3015	35	2
30.	ALL OVER AGAIN	JOHNNY CASH	COL 41251	39	2
31.	WALKING ALONG	DIAMONDS	MER 71366	36	2
32.	LITTLE STAR	ELEGANTS	APT 25005	15	14
33.	THERE GOES MY HEART	JONI JAMES	MGM 12706	38	2
34.	OVER AND OVER	BOBBY DAY	CLASS 229	17	12
35.	TUNNEL OF LOVE	DORIS DAY	COL 41252	--	1
36.	NEED YOU	DONNIE OWENS	GUYDEN 2001	40	2
37.	I'LL WAIT FOR YOU	FRANKIE AVALON	CHAN 1026	--	1
38.	LONESOME TOWN	RICKY NELSON	IMP 5545	--	1
39.	GUALGIONE	PEREZ PRADO	RCA 7337	--	1
40.	FALLIN'	CONNIE FRANCIS	MGM 127013	--	1

NEW RECORDS TO WATCH

ALMOST IN YOUR ARMS Johnny Nash ABC	LOVE IS ALL WE NEED Jimmy Breedlove Epic
ALMOST IN YOUR ARMS Vera Lynn London	LOVE MAKES THE WORLD GO 'ROUND
CAMEO RING Sonny Vito ABC	Perry Como RCA
COME BACK MY LOVE Jerry Butler Abner	MOCKING BIRD Four Lads Columbia
COME ON, LET'S GO Ritchie Valens Del-Fi	MY HEART BELONGS TO ONLY YOU Mary Swan Swan
GOD'S GREATEST GIFT Al Alberts Decca	PALM OF YOUR HAND Dolly Lyon Apollo
HIDEAWAY Four Esquires Paris	PEACHES AND CREAM Larry Williams Specialty
I COULD BE A MOUNTAIN Don Rondo Jubilee	POOR BOY Cardigans Mercury
IT DON'T HURT NO MORE Nappy Brown Savoy	POOR BOY Royal Tones Jubilee
I WILL LOVE YOU Shelby Flint Cadence	ROCK-A-CHA Oscar McLollie Annette Class
LETTER TO AN ANGEL Jimmy Clanton Ace	THERE'S NO TOMORROW Jimmy Nabors Roulette
LOVE IS ALL WE NEED Tommy Edwards MGM	TRICKLE TRICKLE Videos Casino

OFFICIAL

in a three-way tie for first in the ratings. After that event, WIND never again reached the huge numbers it once had under Miller.

What most people don't realize is that even WGN decided to jump on the rock and roll band wagon and began to play the new music. In 1958, WGN, headed by Ward Quaal, had hired a young disc jockey from WLW in Cincinnati and gave him a rock and roll show. Can you imagine hearing Chuck Berry and Bill Haley and the Comets on 720 AM radio every Monday through Friday night from 7 to 11 P.M.? The show was called "The Coca Cola Hi-Fi Club," and it featured none other than Wally Phillips. In later years, Wally told me that while he didn't personally care for rock and roll, he did give it his best shot and he sounded great. The show was dropped a few years later, and Wally went on to bigger and better things at WGN as their morning man.

On the other end of the dial at 1160 AM, WJJD was owned in the early 1950s by department store magnate, Marshall Field. In 1955, he sold the station to the Plough Broadcasting Company. According to Sid Roberts, who was the afternoon DJ on WJJD from 1950 to 1959, when Plough took over and began rocking and rolling, the station was no longer a pleasant place to work. Roberts said that in an effort to create a unified sound, Plough pushed the on-air staff hard to create what they considered to be a well-oiled rock and roll machine. However, WJJD failed for two reasons: one was the same reason that doomed rock and roll radio in the '70s–a lack of well known, DJ personalities; the same old records, and the same limited play list; and, playing those songs over and over. But what probably really doomed the station was a weak signal at night. While they were a 50,000 watt "boomer" during the day, the power dropped to 5,000 watts in the evening and overnight hours. This decision was made to protect another radio station, KSL, located on the same frequency in Salt Lake City. Each time WJJD would go to the FCC asking for a frequency change, KSL's apparent clout at the FCC led to the same negative response. So, at night, with only 5,000 watts of power in their directional radio towers, WJJD was barely audible in some of the Chicago suburbs.

The October 1958 WJJD's "Top Forty Survey" listed *Topsy Part Two* by Cozy Cole as the number one song and *It's All In The Game* by Tommy Edwards in the number two spot. Number three was *Chantilly Lace* by the Big Bopper. In addition, Tommy Dorsey's *Tea For Two Cha Cha* and Jane Morgan's *Day The Rains Came* were also on the chart, while Chicago singer, Nick Noble, had a national hit with *The Bible Tells Me So*. There was still life in the ballads of the '40s and mid-'50s, and that audience was also buying records, but they were slowly being pushed off the charts by the new rock and roll fans. In the late '50s, Ricky Nelson was a cute teenager being showcased on his parents television show, *Ozzie and Harriet*, and his song *Lonesome Town* was gaining teenage girl fans. So was a teenager named Paul Anka with his hit, *Just Young*, and Bobby Darin with *Queen of the Hop*. Each of these songs targeted teenaged girls, and they were buying millions of those records.

Less than four months later, on February 3, 1959, J.P. Richardson, aka, The Big Bopper, along with Buddy Holly and Richie Valens tragically lost their lives in an airplane crash while flying from a record hop in Clear Lake, Iowa. That dance was emceed by a DJ who later went on to be one of the big "rock jocks" at WLS in the 1960s: Bob Hale. Ricky Nelson later lost his life in a plane crash on the way to an appearance, and the same thing would happen in other crashes to such singing stars as Otis Redding, Patsy Cline, Jim Reeves, John Denver, and Jim Croce. As a pilot, I was keenly aware of their deaths, and it was only a few years later, while making appearances in Indiana, that I almost lost my life in two separate airplane flights, both times the result of my own pilot error.

CHICAGO'S TOP STATION
WIND
DIAL 560

TOP 21

WHERE YOU HEAR THE NEW HITS FIRST!

CHICAGO'S OFFICIAL GUIDE TO RECORD POPULARITY
WEEK OF MAY 30, 1958
TOP 21 SINGLES

	Title	Artist	Last Week
1	ALL I HAVE TO DO IS DREAM	Everly Brothers	1
2	JENNIE LEE	Jan & Arnie	8
3	RETURN TO ME	Dean Martin	2
4	DO YOU WANT TO DANCE	Bobby Freeman	9
5	WITCH DOCTOR	David Seville	3
6	JOHNNY B. GOODE	Chuck Berry	5
7	TWILIGHT TIME	The Platters	4
8	WEAR MY RING AROUND YOUR NECK	Elvis Presley	6
9	ZORRO	The Chordettes	12
10	BIG MAN	The Four Preps	16
11	NO CHEMISE, PLEASE	Jerry Granahan	19
12	KEWPIE DOLL	Perry Como	7
13	LET THE BELLS KEEP RINGING	Paul Anka	10
14	NEE NEE NA NA NA NA NU NU	Dickie Doo & Don'ts	9
15	WHOLE WORLD IN HIS HANDS	Laurie London	15
16	PURPLE PEOPLE EATER	Sheb Wooley	--
17	SUGAR MOON	Pat Boone	17
18	ALL THE TIME	Johnny Mathis	13
19	TALK TO ME, TALK TO ME	Little Willie John	20
20	MAKE ME A MIRACLE	Jimmie Rodgers	--
21	CHA-HUA-HUA	The Pets	--
21	LEROY	Jack Scott	--

DOM QUINN

HOWARD MILLER

BERN ALLE

MILO HAMILTON

JOHN DORE

HARVEY'S RECORD SHOP
685 VERNON AVENUE
GLENCOE, ILLINOIS

TOMORROW'S TOPS

	Title	Artist	Label
1	EL RANCHO ROCK	The Champs	Chal
2	PICKIN' ON THE WRONG CHICKEN	The 5 Stars	Hunt
3	DING DONG	McGuire Sisters	Cora
4	WINDY	Paul Gayten	Argo
5	HAPPY FEELING	Debbie Reynolds	Cor.
6	PATRICIA	Perez Prado	RCA
7	TIP TOE THROUGH THE TULIPS	Russ Hamilton	Kapp
8	LITTLE PIXIE	Johnny Pate	Fed.
8	LITTLE PIXIE	Moe Kaufman	Jub.
9	KISSIN' AT THE DRIVE-IN	Gary Shelton	Merc
10	SHINE ON HARVEST MOON	Googie Rene	Clas
11	FOR YOUR PRECIOUS LOVE	Jerry Butler	Falc
12	GOT A MATCH	Daddy-O's	Cabo
12	GOT A MATCH	Frank Gallup	ABC
13	JUDY	Frank Vaughn	Epic
14	OL' MAN RIVER	Earl Grant	Deco
15	BIKINI	The Bikinis	Roul
16	WILLIE & HAND JIVE	John Otis	Cap.
17	THE BETTER TO LOVE YOU	John Janis	Carl
18	A MILLION BOYS	Billy Scott	Cam
19	HIGH SCHOOL CONFIDENTIAL	Jerry Lee Lewis	Sun
20	LITTLE SERENADE	Ted Randazzo	Vik
21	YOUNG AND WARM AND WONDERFUL	Tony Bennett	Col.

Just For The Record . . .
John Doremus

In this day of astrophysics and satellites, etc., it's quite appropriate that ye old lunar system should have its day in the field of popular music. When you look through the current list of favorites at WIND you find Mister Moon's name bantered about quite often. There's Googie Rene's SHINE ON HARVEST MOON; SUGAR MOON by Pat Boone; Percy Faith's nostalgic rendition of SAME OLD MOON; and the Drifter's side of MOONLIGHT BAY. So let us hasten to add, my friendly, when you see that big yellow ball above on these warm spring nights, you'll hear many a tribute to its beauty on Chicago's Top Station . . . WIND!

To Clark
Thanks again
Bee Salways
Dick Clark

In the 1950s, country music singers began to recognize the popularity of rhythm and blues, and they jumped in very early in order to get a piece of the action. There was, of course, Jerry Lee Lewis, and an eight-beat-to-the-bar boogie-woogie, combined with his piano antics. He became even more popular when he appeared on the Steve Allen television show and did his routine where he jumped on the piano and banged around on the keys. Allen got caught up in it, and the scene was soon chaotic. Even after Jerry Lee married his 13-year-old cousin and a lot of people said it was the end of his career, kids just loved his music and overlooked the marriage.

Another star from the '50s was Marty Robbins, whom I first met when he was touring in 1959 with Dick Clark's *Cavalcade of Rock and Roll*. As it turned out, Dick Clark and I share the same birthday and I got to know him well over the years. Marty Robbins, Frankie Avalon, Bobby Rydell, and Fabian were on Dick's tour when I first worked with them at the Eagles Ballroom in Milwaukee. The day after the show, Lee Rothman, the program director at WRIT, mentioned to Frankie Avalon that it was his daughter's 13th birthday and would Frankie mind singing happy birthday to her over the phone? Avalon said, "I've got a better idea. Get her a dozen roses, and then I'll knock on your front door and sing 'Happy Birthday' to her in person. He did and when he gave her a birthday hug, the 13-year-old burst into tears.

A few years later Frankie Avalon fell head over heels in love with a former beauty pageant winner named Kathryn Diebel. They married in January of 1963 and after the wedding they immediately flew to Acapulco Mexico for their honeymoon. Years later Frankie told me the first evening didn't quite turn out the way they had planned. After a romantic dinner and champagne, they went back to their hotel room to prepare for bed. Kathryn changed into her special wedding night negligee, while Frankie was in his briefs. They decided to step outside onto their balcony overlooking Acapulco bay and view the city lights. As they did, the balcony door behind them closed and locked! They began yelling to the people below and all they heard was "No comprende!" After a while when a chill began to set in they decided to yell "Help!" Finally a hotel employee arrived on the scene and opened the balcony door for the blushing bride and shivering groom. It turned out to be the start of a wonderful marriage that later brought about eight kids and numerous grandchildren.

Marty Robbins had recorded his popular song, *A White Sport Coat and A Pink Carnation*, a few months earlier. It was a crossover hit that had been recorded as a country song and included an electric rock and roll guitar sound. When I talked to Marty about it, he told me that he realized he was on to something special. "I recognized that I had the potential to go into the pop field." Then, he recorded *El Paso*, which was a story with a nice rock guitar to it, and followed that song with one called *Don't Worry About Me*, which had a very funky sound. That sound was actually created by pure chance in the recording studio when someone accidentally kicked the guitar amplifier causing it to make a new and special sound—"wah, wah, wah!" Someone said, "Wait a minute. Do that again! Let's create a song using that sound." They kicked the amplifier again, and their response was, "Holy mackerel!" So, they recorded the song called *Don't Worry About Me* with a "wah, wah, wah" sound to it, and it was a hit. It was the beginning of a lot of country and western crossovers, and Ray Charles became a part of that trend in the '60s with his own country and western album. In fact, by the mid to late '50s, lots of singers, including country and western, rhythm and blues, rock, and even the pop artists like Kay Starr and Pat Boone, were making a lot of money by crossing over into rock and roll music.

Many years later, I saw an electrifying show on TV that featured Ray Charles, Jerry Lee Lewis, and Fats Domino on stage at the same time and they were making their pianos "sing."

All three of them had done well through the years, and I recalled a conversation with Fats back in Milwaukee while I was emcee of the *Dick Clark Cavalcade of Rock*. Backstage, Fats and I were talking about the short shelf life of a rock entertainer. He commented to me that it wasn't going to happen to him because while he was making a lot of money in his early years as a star he was also investing most of those earnings in real estate, including apartment buildings in New Orleans. I just hope that his dollars and property survived Hurricane Katrina.

Another star from the '50s was Eddie Fisher. When I first met Eddie, he and I were discussing one of his records. As I recall it, he was in my office at WLS but since he had to leave he said to me, "Let me call you later." I agreed and gave him my home phone number. But, a little while went by and I hadn't received that promised call. About two days later Eddie called and I said to him, "You said that you were going to call me." His response was, "I did. I called your home number twice, but whoever answered the phone just hung up on me." That night, when I got home, I said to my wife, Joan, "Did I get a call from a guy named Eddie Fisher?" She said, "Oh, some fool called twice. I asked him who was calling, and he said, 'This is Eddie Fisher. Can I talk to Clark?' But I didn't believe it was really him, so I just hung up the phone." At that point Eddie had left Debbie Reynolds, and, interestingly enough, Joan said to me, "After what he did by divorcing Debbie for Liz Taylor, I'm glad I hung up on him." Over the years, Fisher would tell me, "That was one of the first times in my life that I was flat out hung up on by a woman."

Of course, the most popular star of the era was Elvis Presley. As noted earlier in the book, ironically, he ignited the boys' interest in his music before the girls. That seemed to be the only time in the 1950s that the boys stepped up to the plate and were the first ones to buy a rock and roll singer's records. Elvis had a motorcycle-kind of appeal and a machismo image that boys really liked. They wanted to emulate him and his style, and they wore leather jackets so they would look cool like Elvis. As for the girls of the '50s, I think he was seen by them as that naughty boy with whom their parents didn't want them to associate, while the boys were in their rebellious mode and were drawn to him.

Interestingly, during the '50s, the man who would later become Elvis' manager, "Colonel" Tom Parker had convinced the popular singer, Eddie Arnold, to let him handle some of Arnold's public relations work. One of the first things that Parker did was during Christmas of 1957 when he had Eddie Arnold send out Christmas cards with a personalized "thank you" on them to every disc jockey in the country. I received one while I was a DJ in West Bend, Wisconsin. I thought it was exciting to get a Christmas card from Eddie Arnold, and I was impressed.

Ironically, when I became a disc jockey in Chicago, Elvis was one of the few rock and roll stars I never met. That occurred because of a disagreement between WLS and his manager, Colonel Parker, who had, at one time, been a circus barker. By the early to mid '60s, Presley had become a very big star. WLS was scheduled to host an Elvis concert at the Chicago Amphitheater around 1964 or 1965, and part of the agreement was for Elvis to make an appearance on WLS that day. But Parker put his foot down and said "no" to the radio appearance, although we were never told why that decision had been made. Gene Taylor told Parker, "If you're not bringing him here, then we're not sponsoring the concert." Well, the "Colonel" seemed not to care about Gene's threat since he had already sold out the Amphitheater and didn't need WLS to promote the appearance. So, Elvis went on the stage without us, and the final score was Elvis—1 and WLS—0. By then, Presley was selling an incredible amount of records and albums, and, in fact, in the early '60s, his sales totaled $75,000 worth of singles and $50,000 worth of albums a day. It was the beginning of a very, very successful career as one of America's music icons.

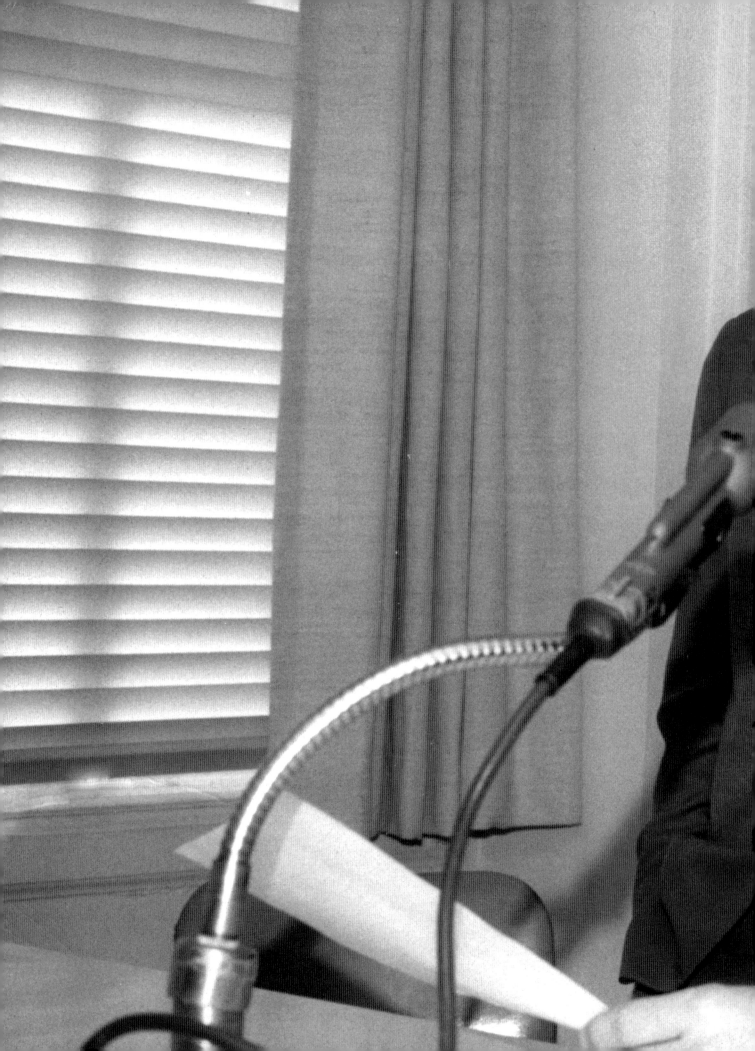

Clark Weber and Eddie Fisher.

Chapter 4
WLS:
The Brigadoon
of Broadcasting

By 1955, many radio stations, including WLS, were feeling the economic pinch of changing music interests. The station had been around since 1924, and its 50,000 watt, clear channel frequency made certain that it was a Midwest mainstay.

The programs on the station at that time included a series of 15-minute live radio shows and the very popular *Saturday Night Barn Dance*. At the time, WLS was owned by the Prairie Farmer Publishing Company and the station had over 190 employees.

While WLS didn't deliver much in the way of profit, the company's publishing division, which dated back to the 1840s, made a lot of money! Then, in the mid-1950s, the American Broadcasting Company (ABC) made a successful offer to Prairie Farmer to buy half the company. By 1959, WLS Radio was operating deep in the red, so ABC offered to buy the other half of Prairie Farmer for a reported $4 million.

Ralph Beaudin was brought in as president and general manager of WLS from another ABC station, and Beaudin, a former US Marine sergeant, operated the station with a firm military style. Sam Holman, who had successfully programmed KQV in Pittsburgh, was the station's program director, and, in May 1960, when WLS went on the air with its new rock and roll format, Holman had a solid lineup of talent. The DJs included: Mort Crowley from WIL in St. Louis; Ed Grennen, who had been with the old WLS, and who was replaced shortly after he arrived by Jim Dunbar, from Detroit, in mid-mornings; Gene Taylor, formerly at WOKY-Milwaukee, in the early afternoon; Holman on the Silver Dollar Survey Show in the afternoon;, followed by the "Wild Italian" Dick Biondi, Art Roberts, and the "East of Midnight Show" with DJ Bob Hale from Peoria. The WLS programming people understood that the core of rock and roll music was all about teenage rebellion, pure and simple. These kids were just coming of age and claiming this music as their own while rebelling from the norm and just loving it. The station followed the credo of "know your market and what appeals to your customers, and you will become rich." The first day that WLS was on the air as a rock station in 1960, it played *Alley Oop* by the Hollywood Argyles nonstop for 24 straight hours. Who ever heard of such a rebellious stunt? But the teenagers loved it, and that introduction of the station really grabbed their attention.

The WLS signal, with its 50,000 watts on a clear channel, reached all over the globe and entertained millions of listeners. Its transmitter was located in Tinley Park, Illinois where some of the neighbors were not all that thrilled about the antenna being situated in their neighborhood...apparently with good reason. It seems that some of the stray radio frequencies from that powerful transmitter, known as stray RF, could and did cause problems. For example, florescent lights in nearby homes would remain lit even after they were switched off. However, as the story goes, the most bizarre event happened on a warm July night when a perspiring, overweight lady sat down on her toilet seat and got the shock of her life. It seems that the toilet seat was made out of aluminum and was just the right dimension to pick up some of that stray RF. The RF shocked her backside, and that caused her to leap up, lose her balance, fall, and break her leg. Of course, WLS paid the medical expenses and also bought her a wooden toilet seat.

As for my career at WLS, it began on September 18, 1961 when I received a call from my old friend, Sam Holman, offering me a job at the station. I was overwhelmed with joy and not a little pride and determined that I had just hit the radio jackpot. Every DJ in the country wanted a shot of working at that station because it was considered to be the "Golden Goose" and the "Mother Lode" of rock and roll radio. Almost 50 years later, it is still easy to describe the direction, care, and camaraderie that existed between management and air staff. Certain station managers are great not because they themselves are superstars, but because they know how to awaken the star that may sleep in each "player" around them. Program directors Sam Holman and Gene Taylor knew how to do that. They directed the programming at WLS with a fair, but firm hand, and simply told us: "We could have hired anyone from around the country for this radio station, but we chose you because you're the best. Do your thing, and if

WLS
silver dollar survey

CHICAGO'S AUTHENTIC RADIO RECORD SURVEY

SEPTEMBER 16, 1961

THIS WEEK			WEEKS PLAYED
1.	MOUNTAIN HIGH	Dick & Dee Dee — Liberty	7
2.	THIS TIME	Troy Shondell — Goldcrest	6
3.	TAKE GOOD CARE OF MY BABY	Bobby Vee — Liberty	5
4.	CHEWING GUM	Lonnie Donegan — Dot	5
5.	MEXICO	Bob Moore — Monument	6
6.	HEART AND SOUL	Jan & Dean — Challenge	6
7.	LET ME BELONG TO YOU	Brian Hyland — ABC Para	10
8.	PRETTY LITTLE ANGEL EYES	Curtis Lee — Dunes	9
9.	STARBRIGHT	Linda Scott — Cam Am	8
10.	MORE MONEY MEDLEY	Four Preps — Capitol	6
11.	WITHOUT YOU	Johnny Tillotson — Cadence	4
12.	MICHAEL	Highwaymen — UA	12
13.	LOVERS ISLAND	Bluejays — Milestone	9
14.	LET THE FOUR WINDS BLOW	Fats Domino — Imperial	7
15.	ASTRONAUT #1	Jose Jimenez — Kapp	4
16.	THE WAY YOU LOOK TONIGHT	Lettermen — Capitol	4
17.	WHO PUT THE BOMP	Barry Mann — ABC Para	8
18.	AMOR	Ben E King — Atco	5
19.	FOOTSTOMPING #1	Flares — Felstad	5
20.	A LITTLE BIT OF SOAP	Jarmels — Laurie	6
21.	JOHNNY WILLOW	Fred Darian — JAF	4
22.	MAGIC MOON	Rays — XYZ	4
23.	KISSING ON THE PHONE	Paul Anka — ABC Para	5
24.	MAGIC IS THE NIGHT	Kathy Young — Indigo	5
25.	BAND OF GOLD	Roomates — Valmor	4
26.	CANDY MAN/CRYING	Roy Orbison — Monument	4
27.	LITTLE SISTER	Elvis Presley — RCA	3
28.	BACK BEAT #1	Rondels — Amy	3
29.	I'M A TELLING YOU	Jerry Butler — VeeJay	5
30.	AS IF I DIDN'T KNOW	Adam Wade — CoEd	4
31.	BEAUTIFUL BABY	Bobby Darin — Atco	2
32.	BLESS YOU	Tony Orlando — Epic	3
33.	HIT THE ROAD JACK	Ray Charles — ABC Para	2
34.	LOOK IN MY EYES	Chantels — Carlton	2
35.	YOU'RE ON TOP	Untouchables — Liberty	4
36.	I'M THANKFUL	Steve Alaimo — Checker	3
37.	NAG	Halos — 7 Arts	3
38.	MY TRUE STORY	Jive Five — Beltone	3
39.	I REALLY LOVE YOU SO	Sterios — Cub	3
40.	SAILOR MAN	Bobby Bare — Fraternity	3

FEATURE ALBUM OF THE WEEK

COME SWING WITH ME — FRANK SINATRA — CAPITOL

Tune in Monday night Sept. 11 for

"EAST OF MIDNIGHT"
and meet personable
CLARK WEBER
Midnight to 5:00 A.M.—Monday thru Saturday

WLS • DIAL 890 • 24 HOURS-A-DAY
ABC RADIO IN CHICAGO

This survey is compiled each week by WLS Radio/Chicago from reports of all record sales gathered from leading record outlets in the Chicagoland area. Hear Gene Taylor play all the SILVER DOLLAR SURVEY hits daily from 3:00 to 6:30 P.M.

you need any corrections, we'll discuss it. Otherwise, entertain them!" Years later, when I became program director at WLS, I remembered those lessons and tried to program the staff accordingly. Regrettably, that mindset seemed to change when another program director assumed the role at the station in the late '60s.

In 1961, my first assignment at WLS was to host the "East of Midnight Show" and I handled that job for 18 months. As I mentioned earlier, since my wife, Joan, and I hadn't sold our new house in Milwaukee, I was commuting between there and Chicago for three hours each way via the North Shore Line. Luckily, at WLS' Christmas Party in December, 1962, Gene Taylor told me that I was getting off the all-night show and becoming the DJ on the "Silver Dollar Survey Show" each afternoon from 4:00 to 7:00 P.M. Gene had taken over when Sam Holman was tapped by WABC in New York to become their program director. Joan and I were overjoyed by the new assignment because it meant decent working hours and more salary. But, that shift didn't last long. Three months later, the WLS morning man, Mort Crowley, became ill and his doctors told him that he could no longer work those early morning hours. So, a short time after becoming afternoon man on the station, I was reassigned to be WLS' morning DJ and I felt that it just couldn't get any better than that!

Our aim was to entertain the audience, and I think we really accomplished that goal. We offered the teenage listeners a fun time with new station jingles, great rock and roll music, and a variety of contests. The morning show appeared to crackle with excitement, personality, and freshness, and the audience response was overwhelming.

While the official sales line was that rock and roll radio stations around the country had a core audience of 18- to 34-year-olds, I think it was a bunch of baloney. The WLS core listeners were made up of kids age 12 and up, and our ratings were measured by that age demographic. We confirmed that conclusion every time we stepped outside the station doors at Michigan and Wacker. In fact, the record hops, concerts, appearances, and our mail all combined to reflect an understanding that we had primarily a young teenage audience that continued to grow in size like wildfire. In fact, Dick Biondi's nighttime audience reached unprecedented numbers that totaled perhaps 80% of Chicago's total nighttime radio listening audience.

None of us ever know when a small act of kindness can nurture a dream. In 1963, a Chicago teenager was scheduled to appear as a guest teen disc jockey on Dick Biondi's Saturday night WLS radio show. At that time, kids would write in to the station and Dick would choose a letter, invite the teen to come in, and he would interview the kid on the air for a few minutes. One night, Dick was ill and Art Roberts sat in for him. Like all teens, the guest DJ was a young man who was both scared and excited to be on WLS that night. Years later and he still hasn't forgotten the thrill because it certainly planted the seed for his career. In fact, you can see him every night on network television across the country hosting a little nationally syndicated program called *Wheel of Fortune*. Yes, his name is Pat Sajak.

The WLS powerful signal was heard in all 50 states and mail poured into the station on a daily basis. That kind of success meant that commercials began to fill the radio log very quickly. According to former WLS salesman, Ed Doody, our spots sold for $200 a minute and we carried 16 spots an hour. On any given day, WLS was bringing in over $50,000 in advertisement revenues! This occurred at a time when the average salesman's salary was $12,000 a year. As I recall, one of the station's unhappiest salesmen was a guy named Mike Ditka. Mike finally quit his sales job at the station when he received a call from Bears' owner, George Halas, with an offer to become an assistant coach with the team, which, of course, he accepted. And, after

Clark Weber's high-ranking "wake-up" show starts the day in fast tempo on the Bright Sound of Chicago radio, WLS. Known in the broadcasting business as a "real professional," Clark is a man who gives conscientious attention to detail and technique. His morning program is a popular mixture of humor, lively music, traffic reports, news and the weather.

Clark's broadcasting career was launched when he landed an announcer's job with WBKV in West Bend, Wis., later becoming news director. He moved to WRIT in Milwaukee in 1958 where he hosted during prime early-morning-show time. In September, 1960, he took over the "East of Midnight" program on WLS.

At home in Evanston, Ill., Clark says he worked out his engineering frustrations on a ham radio set. Flying, home movies of his four daughters, and literally hundreds of personal appearances for civic and charitable events round out a busy schedule.

Clark is a man who walks and talks with a smile, and it's a happy voice that fast-paces the morning show. "I love this shift," Clark says, with typical candor. Thousands of listeners agree with him.

CLARK WEBER... EARLY MORNING

ABC OWNED RADIO STATIONS

WABC NEW YORK • WXYZ DETROIT • KQV PITTSBURGH • WLS CHICAGO • KGO SAN FRANCISCO • KABC LOS ANGELES

left to right
Bernie Allen, Don Phillips, Art Roberts, Clark Weber, Ron Riley, and Dex Card.

some years with the Bears, he left for an assistant coach position with the Dallas Cowboys before Halas hired him back to the Bears as head coach. Of course, Ditka would lead the Bears to a victory in Super Bowl XX in 1986.

After beginning my years at WLS, I began a separate career as an on-air voice talent doing radio and television commercials. It all began on July 4, 1963 when I had the good fortune of being introduced to Shirley Hamilton, a Chicago talent agent extraordinaire. She commented to me that she had heard my voice on WLS and thought that I had a special talent to do commercials. In fact, she suggested that I stop by her office some day to discuss the possibilities. Two days later, we met and I soon became a member of her "stable of voice talents." I began getting voice work, but nothing that one could consider earth shattering. However, one day, I received a request to come to a "cattle call" audition for a fast food commercial. A "cattle call" is when an ad agency contacts a talent agency and requests that they send over perhaps 10 to 20 of their best voices who might fit the agency's need for a particular radio or television commercial. When you arrive at the audition, you are given a copy of a script to study. Then, one by one, you are requested to come into the studio, stand before the advertising agency talent director, and give your best shot at reading the commercial. The guy who was running the audition that day had a nasty reputation of responding to talent with a hair trigger temper.

After I read the 30-second commercial, there was a moment of silence before he proceeded to unload a series of negative comments on me. In an explosive voice, the director said to me, "If I wanted some guy who sounded like a damned disc jockey, I would have asked for one! Now, get out of here and send in the next person." I left that audition embarrassed, angry, and upset. Of course I sounded like a disc jockey since I had been one for over 10 years—and a good one. But, I realized that, just maybe, I didn't sound like a "believable" person.

I immediately got the name of one of the best voice coaches in Chicago and, several months and many hours later, the coach "knocked" the disc jockey style out of my voice and taught me how to properly read a commercial. As a result, down through the years, listeners and viewers have heard me as everything from the voice of "Mr. Clean," to a portrayal of a doctor for Blue Cross, and hundreds of other commercials. Years later, when I created my own advertising agency, I remembered the shoddy treatment I had received at that early audition and never treated anyone seeking a job doing an ad with anything but kindness and respect.

Speaking of commercials, we can now put to rest, once and for all, one of the greatest urban myths related to Dick Biondi and the supposed story of why he got fired from WLS. To this day, I still run into people who tell me the tired tale that they were listening the night Biondi supposedly told an off-color story on the air that caused him to be fired. The undeniable fact is that it just didn't happen. I was there and became an eyewitness to the incident. In fact, here's what did happen. There was a disagreement between Dick and WLS management over the increase in the commercial load during his show. He had monstrous ratings, and it seemed that every sponsor in the country wanted to reach that audience and was willing to pay any price that WLS would charge for commercial time on his show. As it turned out, an American Dairy Association's advertisement happened to be the one additional ad that broke the camel's back.

Biondi went on the air one night in 1963, saw the added commercial, and became irate. Armend Belli, the WLS sales manager, tried to calm him down, but Dick was very unhappy. I had just come off my "Silver Dollar Survey Show" when I heard what appeared to be a loud commotion in the hall. Dick was making it clear to Armend, in no uncertain terms, that he didn't want to have so many advertisements because they were forcing him to interrupt the flow of music on his program. Program Director Gene Taylor intervened and tried to calm down the situation, and finally suggested to Dick that he go home and just cool off. Biondi did go home, but the next day, May 2, 1963, three years to the day he had begun at WLS, he was fired. Station manager Ralph Beaudin had tried to sort out the situation, but ended up firing Dick.

It was highly regrettable for Dick, and for WLS, because he had become so popular, with his own national audience, and was our "Pied Piper." The kids loved Dick, and his listeners have always been very loyal because Biondi prided himself on looking out for his listeners and he felt an obligation to take care of their welfare, (i.e., just too many commercials). However, WLS resisted Biondi's reaction to the added commercials and made clear to him that the station was determined to maintain its position on the number of advertisements. It was a situation that had gotten out of hand, and Dick's career was affected by the event. So, simply put: there was no dirty story...just a misguided understanding of the situation. And, despite his great popularity at WLS, Dick was fired by the station. Years later, Biondi did return to Chicago at WCFL, then, later at WJMK, and finally at WZZN (now WLS.FM) where he holds forth today. Dick Biondi has also been inducted into three halls of fame: Rock and Roll; the Radio Hall of Fame; and Museum of Broadcast Communications.

When it comes to the salaries of WLS DJs, I think that we were always well paid thanks to the fact that the American Federation of Television and Radio Artists (AFTRA) had a union contract with Chicago's major radio stations. The union scale starting salary for a WLS DJ in 1961 was $32,500 a year. I will always be thankful for the unions because radio stations of every stripe could and did screw the DJs out of money whenever they were able to do it and the stations resented the power of unions. The AFTRA and SAG (Screen Actors Guild) were very hard nosed in dealing with the stations. However, thanks to the unions' unstinting efforts on our behalf, some of us received excellent pensions and health care in our later years. So, this advice to those who want a career in radio: join AFTRA and SAG; hire an attorney you can trust; and be certain to have a good insurance agent and CPA. You'll sleep better at night and have a great nest egg when you hang up your earphones!

Some of the DJs were able to work their way up the salary scale from making $45,000 to as much as $60,000 a year, depending on their on-air shift, with the morning man making the most money. By the mid to late '60s, a few salaries even increased to $75,000 a year. Then, there were the paid appearances, which became a non-stop phenomenon for DJs. Record hop and speaking appearances of $250 to $350 per night were also common in those years. Since I had already learned how to fly, I was able to use a small airplane to cover a four state area, week in and week out for such appearances. The demand for appearances was such that some disc jockeys ended up adding to their annual salaries by earning another $20,000 to $45,000 a year on the side. The demand for WLS personalities was so great in those days that, in fact, our traffic reporter, a Chicago police officer named Vic Petrolis, was needed to do record hops on a regular basis.

It is ironic that today's morning man or woman in Chicago radio would consider our salaries from the '60s to be "chump change." A paycheck for them probably ranges from $400,000 to a $1 million a year, but I will bet that they don't have as much pure fun as we did more than 40 years ago. To put those 1960s dollars in proper perspective, gasoline at that time was 28 cents a gallon, and Mr. Norm's Grand Spaulding Dodge in Chicago, a sponsor on WLS, was advertising Dodge Charger 425 Hemi-Powered muscle cars for $3,695. Some of those same cars today command prices of over $90,000. Aren't you sorry you sold yours?

Clark Weber

"The WLS programming people understood that the core of rock and roll music was all about teenage rebellion, pure and simple. These kids were just coming of age and claiming this music as their own while rebelling from the norm and just loving it."

"We offered the teenage listeners a fun time with new station jingles, great rock and roll music, and a variety of contests."

The WLS Farm Show crew, including Charles "Homer Bill," Clark Weber, Tom Fouts (aka "Captain Stubby").

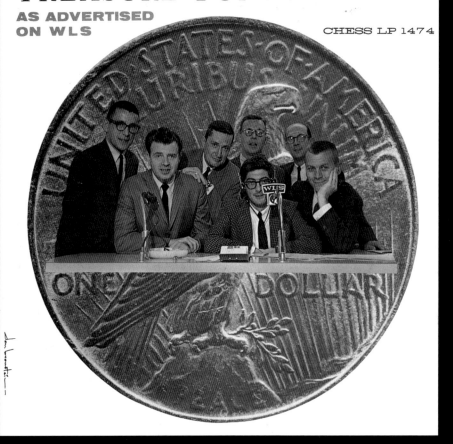

TREASURE TUNES FROM THE VAULT

AS ADVERTISED ON WLS

CHESS LP 1474

LP-1474

TREASURE TUNES

Chess LP 1474
high-fidelity

LP-1474

TREASURE TUNES

Treasure Tunes from The Vault
as advertised on WLS

Off The Record

Side 1

	Time
A THOUSAND STARS (Kathy Young) (Pearson: Challenge Music—BMI)	2:48
LA BAMBA (Ritchie Valens) (Valens: Keno Music—BMI)	2:03
BUT I DO (Clarence Henry) (Guidry, Gayten: Arc Music—BMI)	2:15
SO FINE (The Fiestas) (Gribble: Maureen Music—BMI)	2:20
STAY (Maurice Williams & The Zodiacs) (M. Williams: Windsong Music—BMI)	1:50
SWEET LITTLE SIXTEEN (Chuck Berry) (C. Berry Music Inc.: Arc Music—BMI)	2:37
	Total Time 13:53

Side 2

	Time
TONIGHT I FELL IN LOVE (The Tokens) (Margo, Medress: Halkay Music—BMI)	1:42
LAVENDER BLUE (Sammy Turner) (L. Morey, E. Daniel: Joy Music Inc.—ASCAP)	2:13
MONEY (Barrett Strong) (B. Gordy, J. Bradford: Jobete Music Co.—BMI)	2:33
OH JULIE (The Crescendos) (Excellorec Music—BMI)	2:35
BOOK OF LOVE (Monotones) (Davis, Malone, Patrick: Arc Music/Keel—BMI)	2:15
LONG, LONELY NIGHTS (Lee Andrews & The Hearts) (Andrews, Henderson: Arc Music/G & H—BMI)	2:50
	Total Time 14:08

Cover: Don Bronstein

TONIGHT I FELL IN LOVE (The Tokens) through the courtesy of Gertrude Gottesfield.

STAY (Maurice Williams & The Zodiacs) by arrangement with Herald Records.

CHESS PRODUCING CORP. • 2120 SOUTH MICHIGAN AVENUE • CHICAGO 16, ILLINOIS

WLS
The bright sound of Chicago Radio

SILVER DOLLAR SURVEY
Chicago's Official Radio Record Survey

THIS WEEK	JANUARY 25, 1963		WEEKS PLAYED
1.	HEY PAULA	Paul & Paula — Phillips	7
2.	WALK RIGHT IN	Rooftop Singers — Vanguard	6
3.	GO AWAY LITTLE GIRL	Steve Lawrence — Columbia	11
4.	THE NIGHT HAS A THOUSAND EYES	Bobby Vee — Liberty	9
5.	CAST YOUR FATE TO THE WIND	Vince Guaraldi Trio — Fantasy	5
6.	I SAW LINDA YESTERDAY	Dickey Lee — Smash	9
7.	FROM A JACK TO A KING	Ned Miller — Faber	9
8.	HE'S SURE THE BOY I LOVE	The Crystals — Philles	5
9.	RUBY BABY	Dion — Columbia	4
10.	MY DAD	Paul Peterson — Colpix	9
11.	WALK LIKE A MAN	Four Seasons — Vee Jay	3
12.	UP ON THE ROOF	Drifters — Atlantic	10
13.	LOOP DE LOOP	Johnny Thunder — Diamond	6
14.	WHAT TO DO WITH LAURIE	Mike Clifford — UA	8
15.	THE 2,000 POUND BEE (Part 2)	Ventures — Dolton	6
16.	LITTLE TOWN FLIRT	Del Shannon — Big Top	5
17.	IT'S UP TO YOU	Rick Nelson — Imperial	8
18.	PUDDIN N' TAIN	Alley Cats — Philles	7
19.	BONNIE DO	Johnny Cooper — Ermine	7
20.	CINNAMON CINDER	Pastel Six — Zen	7
21.	PROUD	Johnny Crawford — Del Fi	6
22.	THE BIRD	The Dutones — Columbia	4
23.	I WANNA BE AROUND	Tony Bennett — Columbia	5
24.	YOU'RE THE REASON I'M LIVING	Bobby Darin — Capitol	3
25.	COME BACK LITTLE GIRL	Ronnie Rice — IRC	4
26.	THE BALLAD OF JED CLAMPETT	L. Flatt & E. Scruggs — Columbia	7
27.	TROUBLE IN MIND	Aretha Franklin — Columbia	5
28.	GREENBACK DOLLAR	Kingston Trio — Capitol	3
29.	WHAT WILL MARY SAY	Johnny Mathis — Columbia	3
30.	THE POPEYE WADDLE	Don Covay — Cameo	4
31.	BACHELOR MAN	Johnny Cymbal — Kedlen	4
32.	STRANGE I KNOW	Marvelettes — Tamla	8
33.	YOU'VE REALLY GOT A HOLD ON ME	Miracles — Tamla	5
34.	RHYTHM OF THE RAIN	Cascades — Valiant	4
35.	FLY ME TO THE MOON	Joe Harnell — Kapp	2
36.	SEAGRAMS	The Viceroys — Bethlehem	4
37.	LET ME GO THE RIGHT WAY	Supremes — Motown	3
38.	JAVA	Floyd Cramer — RCA	3
39.	WILD WEEKEND	The Rebels — Swan	2
40.	WHO STOLE THE KEESHKA	Matys Bros. — Select	2

FEATURED ALBUMS
SINATRA — BASIE — REPRISE
WALK RIGHT IN — THE ROOFTOP SINGERS — VANGUARD
OUR MAN AROUND THE WORLD — PAUL ANKA — RCA

Don't miss the fun with

Dick Biondi

9 to Midnight — Monday thru Sunday

WLS • DIAL 890 • 24 HOURS-A-DAY
ABC RADIO IN CHICAGO

This survey is compiled each week by WLS Radio/Chicago from reports of all record sales gathered from leading record outlets in the Chicagoland area. Hear Clark Weber play all the SILVER DOLLAR SURVEY hits daily from 3:00 to 6:30 P.M.

WLS
The bright sound of Chicago Radio

SILVER DOLLAR SURVEY
Chicago's Official Radio Record Survey

THIS WEEK	MAY 24, 1963		WEEKS PLAYED
* 1.	IT'S MY PARTY	Leslie Gore — Mercury	6
* 2.	TWO FACES HAVE I	Lou Christie — Roulette	9
* 3.	YOU CAN'T SIT DOWN	Dovells — Parkway	8
* 4.	RA DO RON RON	Crystals — Philles	8
5.	FOOLISH LITTLE GIRL	Shirelles — Scepter	8
6.	IF YOU WANNA BE HAPPY	Jimmy Soul — SPQR	10
7.	I LOVE YOU BECAUSE	Al Martino — Capitol	8
* 8.	SURFIN U.S.A.	Beach Boys — Capitol	8
* 9.	CAN'T GET USED TO LOSING YOU	Andy Williams — Columbia	12
*10.	HOT PASTRAMI	Dartells/Joey Dee — Dot/Roulette	7
*11.	LOSING YOU	Brenda Lee — Decca	8
*12.	WHAT A GUY	Raindrops — Jubilee	8
*13.	SUKAYAKA	Kyu Sakamoto — Capitol	8
*14.	STING RAY	Routers — WB	5
*15.	TAMOURE	Bill Justis — Smash	6
*16.	HERE I STAND	Ripchords — Columbia	6
*17.	EIGHTEEN YELLOW ROSES	Bobby Darin — Capitol	5
*18.	EL WATUSI	Ray Barreto — Tico	6
*19.	THE BOY I'M GONNA MARRY	Darlene Love — Philles	8
20.	DO IT RAT NOW	Bill Black Combo — Hi	4
*21.	HELLO STRANGER	Barbara Lewis — Atlantic	4
*22.	KILLER JOE	Rocky Fellers — Scepter	7
*23.	STILL	Bill Anderson — Decca	3
*24.	WILDWOOD DAYS	Bobby Rydell — Cameo	4
*25.	I'M SAVING MY LOVE	Skeeter Davis — RCA	5
*26.	LET'S GO STEADY AGAIN	Neil Sedaka — RCA	5
*27.	PRISONER OF LOVE	James Brown — King	4
*28.	BIRDLAND	Chubby Checker — Parkway	4
*29.	SAD SAD BOY AND GIRL	Impressions — ABC Para	3
*30.	ONE FINE DAY	Chiffons — Laurie	4
*31.	IF MY PILLOW COULD TALK	Connie Francis — MGM	4
*32.	THOSE LAZY HAZY CRAZY DAYS OF SUMMER	Nat Cole — Capitol	6
33.	THE LOVE OF MY MAN	Theola Kilgore — Serock	5
*34.	THE BOUNCE	Olympics — Tri Disc	4
*35.	MY SUMMER LOVE	Ruby & Romantics — Kapp	4
*36.	POOR LITTLE RICH GIRL	Steve Lawrence — Columbia	4
*37.	GYPSY WOMAN	Rick Nelson — Decca	3
*38.	MANHATTEN SPIRITUAL	Santo & Johnny — Can-Am	3
*39.	I'M MOVIN ON	Matt Lucas — Smash	3
*40.	GEE LITTLE GIRL	Nick Noble — Liberty	3

FEATURED ALBUMS
JULIE LONDON — LIBERTY
FOR YOUR SWEET LOVE — RICK NELSON — DECCA

Swing Along with

Clark Weber

3:00 to 6:30 P.M.—Monday thru Friday
3 to 6 P.M. Saturday and Sunday

WLS • DIAL 890 • 24 HOURS-A-DAY
ABC RADIO IN CHICAGO

This survey is compiled each week by WLS Radio/Chicago from reports of all record sales gathered from leading record outlets in the Chicagoland area. Hear Clark Weber play all the SILVER DOLLAR SURVEY hits daily from 3:00 to 6:30 P.M. *Denotes record first heard in Chicago on WLS.

I remember when the WLS Payroll Department asked me to speak to one our DJs, Dex Card, about the fact that he wasn't cashing his payroll checks. It seemed that Dex was making so much money from record hops that he was stuffing his payroll checks in his desk drawer and forgetting to cash them. Dex was the DJ for the "Silver Dollar Survey Show" in the afternoons during the mid to late '60s. He was a good looking guy, and his looks weren't lost on the teenaged girls who flocked around him at personal appearances asking for his autograph. Once, at a South Bend, Indiana record hop, a young lady wearing a strapless sun dress asked Dex to autograph her bare shoulder. He was kind enough to oblige, but got carried away and by the time he was done writing "Thanks for listening to WLS" he had written across part of her chest. The next day, while the girl was trying to scrub off the autograph, her mother discovered Dex's name on her anatomy. The girl's mother immediately contacted ABC and WLS, and there was hell to pay.

That same year, as part of the "WLS Super Summer," complete with the WLS "Treasure Truck," the station introduced the "WLS Beach Patrol." The concept was quite simple. Each Saturday afternoon, two WLS DJs, armed with $100 in silver dollars and copies of WLS Silver Dollar music surveys would roam Chicago beaches looking for people whose radios were tuned to our station. We would introduce ourselves, award silver dollars to the winning listeners, and of course, sign autographs. Dex and I were on patrol one Saturday afternoon during the summer at Oak Street Beach when Dex spied a lovely young lady lying on her stomach sunning herself and listening to WLS. He also noticed that she had undone the straps on her top to get a more even tan. Dex and I knelt down in front of her, introduced ourselves, and awarded her the silver dollar. The girl was so surprised and overwhelmed because we had come face to face with her that, as she raised up to accept the silver dollar, she forgot that her top was unhooked. Of course her breasts tumbled out in front of us. In recalling that story to other DJs, Dex pointed out that it kind of made you proud to know that we were helping a lovely young woman get such an even summer tan.

On the subject of autographs, it has always amazed me that by the time some show business or sports lout reaches a position of notoriety, they either refuse to be bothered with an autograph request or they sign them under protest. The real reason for the autograph is that the fan is recognizing the "star" as someone important enough to warrant the autograph. In other words, it's not about the "star," it's about the fan and a brief claim to fame. So, I have always strongly believed that you sign the requested autograph and be grateful that they're fans. They pay the salary, and, besides, some day they'll stop asking!

Even though big money was being made by the WLS DJs, there were a few who throughout the station's history spent the dollars like they would never end. They were stars, but, in truth, the life expectancy of a typical WLS DJ was, on the average, only 3.2 years. So, for many DJs it was a very brief ride. There were few exceptions to the rule: I was there 8 1/2 years, while Art Roberts stayed for 11 years. As it turned out, Larry Lujack had the longest run, first at WLS for four years, and then returning five years later for another 13 years at the station. I recall that one of the WLS DJs was forever buying things on a whim. He would spend like a drunken sailor on a Saturday night! You never knew what kind of car he was driving, but he topped the car purchases one night when he went to the annual Chicago boat show and bought a boat even though he had never been on the water!

SUPER SUMMER LIVES

SUPER SUMMER

WLS

Clark Weber with WLS Station Manager, Gene Taylor.

Clark Weber with a Playboy Bunny at WLS' "B" Studio.

Chapter 5
WLS and
The Fun Years

I became the WLS program director in 1965 and was both flattered to work with a smooth running, first class management team, and a bit taken aback. Even though I had no experience in radio management when Gene Taylor was moved up to operations director, he asked me to take on the task, all the while providing assurances that he would work with me until I grew confident in the job.

While I was no Jack Welch (later CEO of General Electric), I did have experience as a Navy petty officer and learned that if I took care of my people they would take care of the "store. "When I made the decision to accept the position, it certainly wasn't for the money since the job only paid another $250 a week. And, it meant that not only did I get up at 2:30 A.M. to be the DJ on the WLS morning show each Monday through Saturday from 6 to 10 A.M., including making the preparations for the show, but I would begin dealing with the questions, problems, and promotional challenges of being the station's program director. Thanks to the help of my two secretaries, Maxine Brannigan and Darlene Carr, an enormous amount of time was spent meeting with various record promotion people and listening to their pitches for new records. I allotted the promotion people 15 minutes each over a period of three days every week to promote their new records. Then, on Friday, the new weekly play list came out at 3:00 P.M., the new "Silver Dollar Survey" was released, and, on Monday, the whole process was repeated all over again.

In order for me to select records for the play list, I had to hear a certain hit quality and something that had a "hook" which I thought the kids would find interesting. The selection was also based, to some degree, on what was happening to those songs in the smaller radio markets, and the record promotion men would provide me with additional information about how the songs were moving in those other markets. There were times I got burned in my choices, because I would hear "hit" and it wouldn't happen, and, of course there were the other times when I didn't recognize a hit record and it became very popular. For example, I really missed it on one song by the Mommas and the Poppas called *California Dreaming*. I thought it was a West Coast record and was late by a week in programming it on WLS.

Otis Redding was one of those soul singers who struggled most of his musical life. He once complained to a fellow musician that life on the road singing where ever he could make a buck was hard on him. Plus his family thought he was wasting his time as a singer and didn't respect his career. He decided to write a song about that struggle and recorded it in 1965. While it made the R&B charts hitting number #4 nationwide, it sputtered its way to only number #35 on the pop charts and it promptly died. WLS never played the song. In late 1967 Redding finally hit the big time when he recorded the song, *Sitting on the Dock of the Bay*. Three days later at age 26 Redding died in a plane crash. His chartered twin engine Beechcraft smashed into Lake Mendota while attempting to land at the Madison Wisconsin airport.

What you may not have known was that Redding's real success as a singer came from that song about his career struggle he had written a few years earlier and was all but forgotten. In 1966 a singer decided to include that song in her new album and Otis became a very wealthy man. For you see the singer was Aretha Franklin and Otis's song was *Respect*!

A record myth started by a disgruntled employee continues to this day regarding Aretha's hit record *Respect*. The claim is that as the WLS Program Director I didn't play that hit single long enough. Not True. It debuted on the Silver Dollar Survey on May 5, 1967 and it peaked at #10 on June 2, 1967 and then began to fade. The song spent a total of eight weeks on the WLS charts. While the song hit #1 nationally, the Chicago audience didn't feel that strongly about it. Even on the WCFL charts, the song only reached its peak at #7..

Another source for determining a hit song was to sometimes take obscure records to record hops and watch the kids' reactions to the music. Of course, other stations around the country would monitor our music because if WLS played a song, our competition would immediately jump on it. The promoters also used that information to get support for their songs at other radio stations by referring to the fact that WLS was playing the record.

After I took the new job, my schedule was such that I would get home around 3:00 or 4:00 P.M. just in time to play with our four young daughters, chat with Joan, eat dinner, and get under the covers at 7:30 P.M., the same time the kids went to bed. In addition, the record hop and personal appearances continued nonstop, and that meant at least one or two such events every week. When I made those appearances, I would get home around 1:00 A.M., sleep for a short time, and then go back to the station for another day's work. I was thankful that Joan shouldered most of the parental load because I wasn't around that much. At the same time, my freelance commercial voice work was taking off and I soon discovered that I had begun spreading myself much too thin. It became so much of a grind that only one year after I took the program director job at WLS, I made the decision to inform Gene Taylor that the dual role of being on the air and working as PD was much too hard on me and my family. I asked him to consider finding another program director. Much to my relief, one year later, ABC did hire another person for that role, but it turned out to be a decision that I would later regret. When it came to hiring disc jockeys, WLS maintained an updated "hot list" of national DJs who showed a lot of promise. This information was compiled from secret "air checks," audition tapes, and the all-important promotion men who called on radio stations throughout the country while peddling their records. Many of them knew which DJs were good, bad, hard to handle, and trustworthy. When the time came that we needed another disc jockey, we weren't caught "flat footed," because we knew who we might want to hire.

When Dick Biondi suddenly left WLS in 1963, we quickly reached out to Ron Riley, an old friend and DJ whom I had known in Milwaukee. Riley was working at WOKY, and we asked him to do Don Phillips' "East of Midnight Show" for two weeks while Don was on vacation. It served as a trial by fire, and because Ron sounded great he was offered a full-time job at WLS. Shortly after he came on board, Riley and I met to discuss a promotional idea that had worked well during the 1930s and 1940s and which I felt could be used successfully again. Radio icons Jack Benny and Fred Allen had their own network radio shows during those years, and they would take pot shots at each other on the air. The audiences had eaten it up, so Riley and I decided to try to create the same type of "feud." It was the perfect way to get his huge nighttime teen audience to dial into my morning show and hear me say something bad about Riley, feed my morning ratings, and vice versa.

For example, Riley told his listening audience that I was a jerk of a boss and that if you spelled "boss" backwards it became "double s.o.b." He told his fans that "old baldy locks" was posing as a summer blond thanks to a yellow magic marker. Ron had also created an alter ego named "Bruce Lovely" who helped to further fuel the controversy. I would occasionally either go on his show and bawl him out or leave a memo that would infuriate his audience. For example, about that time, the Beatles had descended on the American entertainment world and teenage girls quickly fell in love with the "Moptop Four." To compound our so-called controversy, I announced that I considered the Dave Clark Five a far superior group of singers in comparison with the Beatles, and the kids went bananas!

CLASS OF SERVICE

This is a fast message unless its deferred character is indicated by the proper symbol.

WESTERN UNION

TELEGRAM

W. P. MARSHALL, PRESIDENT

SF-1201 (4-60)

SYMBOLS

DL=Day Letter

NL=Night Letter

LT=International Letter Telegram

The filing time shown in the date line on domestic telegrams is LOCAL TIME at point of origin. Time of receipt is LOCAL TIME at point of destination

YCA115 (33)(17)BB290

N EJA044 PD EJ NEWYORK NY 19 508PEDT

1965 JUL 19 PM 4 37

CLARK WEBER

RADIO STATION WLS CHGO

DEAR CLARK: CONGRATULATIONS REGARDS

JOHNNY TILLOTSON

(10).

CLASS OF SERVICE

This is a fast message unless its deferred character is indicated by the proper symbol.

WESTERN UNION

TELEGRAM

W. P. MARSHALL, PRESIDENT

SF-1201 (4-60)

SYMBOLS

DL=Day Letter

NL=Night Letter

LT=International Letter Telegram

The filing time shown in the date line on domestic telegrams is LOCAL TIME at point of origin. Time of receipt is LOCAL TIME at point of destination

YCA116 (35)(11)BA268

1965 JUL 19 PM 4 37

N EJA035 PD EJ NEW YORK NY 19 501PEDT

CLARK WEBER

RADIO STATION WLS CHGO

DEAR CLARK: WE "BLOKES" WISH YOU A WONDERFUL WORLD

HERMAN'S HERMITS

(04).

CLASS OF SERVICE

This is a fast message unless its deferred character is indicated by the proper symbol.

WESTERN UNION

TELEGRAM

W. P. MARSHALL, PRESIDENT

SF-1201 (4-60)

SYMBOLS

DL=Day Letter

NL=Night Letter

LT=International Letter Telegram

The filing time shown in the date line on domestic telegrams is LOCAL TIME at point of origin. Time of receipt is LOCAL TIME at point of destination

1965 JUL 19 PM 4 42

CHICAGO ILL

YCA122 (40)(17)BA277

N EJA045 PD EJ NEWYORK NY 19 511PEDT

CLARK WEBER

RADIO STATION WLS CHGO

BRING IT ON HOME REGARDS

THE ANIMALS

(12).

CLASS OF SERVICE

This is a fast message unless its deferred character is indicated by the proper symbol.

WESTERN UNION

TELEGRAM

W. P. MARSHALL, PRESIDENT

SF-1201 (4-60)

SYMBOLS

DL=Day Letter

NL=Night Letter

LT=International Letter Telegram

The filing time shown in the date line on domestic telegrams is LOCAL TIME at point of origin. Time of receipt is LOCAL TIME at point of destination

1965 JUL 30 PM 4 46

YCA110 (44)(35)LA231

L HDA300 CGN PD 6 EXTRA FAX HOLLYWOOD CALIF 30 231P PDT

CLARK WEBER

WLS RADIO STATION CHGO

CONGRATULATIONS ON YOUR NEW APPOINTMENT. WE KNOW YOU WILL DO A FANTASTIC JOB

FRED FLINTSTONE HUCKLEBERRY HOUND YOGI BEAR DON BOHANAN

(35).

Clark Weber preflighting
the plane at Sky Harbor Airport
in Northbrook.

"Ron Riley and I decided to try to create a "feud." It was the perfect way to get his huge nighttime teen audience to dial into my morning show and hear me say something bad about Riley, feed my morning ratings, and vice versa."

It wasn't simply the "theater of the mind" at work, and it worked beyond our wildest dreams. At appearances, Ron's audience would yell out for him to "say something bad about Weber!" WLS also had an on-air promotion called the "Emperor Weber's Commandos" that quickly became very popular. Listeners were told that if they sent a stamped, self-addressed envelope to WLS, the station would send them a Lieutenant's commission in "Weber's Commandos." We sent out over 300,000 of those "commissions," and, to this day, I'm asked to autograph the commissions. Riley countered with his "Riley's Rebel Raiders" and people actually took sides in this feud to the point where Ron and I couldn't be seen dining together. Everywhere we went the other side was represented and our listening audience became wound up tighter than a cheap watch.

One night, while appearing in Champaign, Illinois, and after accidentally bouncing my airplane while landing at the Champaign Airport, I received a communication from the control tower: "Wait until Riley hears about this!" Then, another time, while visiting Peoria for a record hop, two cops came on stage, put me in handcuffs, drove me out onto a lonely road, and told me to get out of the squad car. As they drove away they shouted, "We're Riley's Rebel Raiders." Lucky for me, a few minutes later they came back to pick me up. In 1966, the Armed Forces Radio Network called us in and asked Riley and me to tape a show for the GIs over in 'Nam. We "took a bite out of each other," played a little music, and it was a huge success. Today that tape is considered by many to be a WLS classic.

Our feud served as an opportunity for the audience to become directly involved in the radio station...and they did just that. WLS also created the same reaction from our listeners when they introduced the "WLS Personality Magazine" which featured pictures of each of the deejays and their families. We had an initial print run of 50,000 copies of the magazine, but when the demand hit 150,000, we stopped printing it because of the unexpected cost of production. The same thing happened with the WLS Record Album.

Requests for personal appearances came from all over the Midwest. If one's health could handle the stress, you could be emceeing record hops or concerts every night of the week. In order to cover the states of Illinois, Indiana, Michigan, and Wisconsin, I began flying my own plane. It meant that I could roam far and wide and still be home by 1:30 A.M. and in bed for a short two-hour nap before going back on the air.

However, one summer night in 1964, the fatigue of my schedule finally caught up with me. I had just finished a Wednesday night record hop at the Lake Tippecanoe Ballroom in Warsaw, Indiana about midnight, and soon after, I slid into the cockpit of my twin engine Piper Comanche and headed back to Chicago. As I flew over Knox, Indiana and began heading north, I turned on the autopilot and relaxed. I didn't realize how tired I was and fell sound asleep at the controls. The autopilot kept the plane on course and it continued to drone along at 175 mph on a northerly course. I estimate that I was asleep for perhaps 25 minutes, long enough so that the plane had headed out over the middle of Lake Michigan. When we hit a slight air pocket, the bump woke me up. Talk about panic, I didn't know where I was, and when I looked around it was "darker than a hooker's heart." Fortunately, there was plenty of fuel in the plane and when I took a radio bearing I discovered that I was just south and east of Milwaukee. When I eventually landed back in the Chicago area, I vowed that from then on, and especially if I was doing personal appearances at night, I would always fly with a copilot.

In 1964, when Ford introduced its first Mustangs, their ad agency, J. Walter Thompson, decided it would be a good idea to do something different with their commercials. They asked me to simply talk about the car on my morning show... but they carried it one step further.

Art Roberts "polishing my Chrome Dome."

"The program director is responsible for everything that goes on the air, including the music. The job also involves making sure that the station doesn't lose its license because of what is said or played on the air, and that included songs with suggestive lyrics. That was easy in the '50s and '60s, but as we entered the mid '60s, some lyrics began to cross the line."

left to right
**Don Phillips, Ron Riley,
Larry Lujack, Art Roberts,
Clark Weber, and
Bernie Allen.**

left to right
**Ron Riley, Don Phillips,
Bernie Allen, Art Roberts,
and Clark Weber.**

Gene Taylor joins Clark Weber for a luncheon meeting at the Brief Encounter restaurant on Michigan Avenue.

Every 30 days, for a year, the deal was that they would give me a new and different Ford Mustang to drive. Not only did I experience the car and talk about it, but the audience saw me driving one and it certainly helped Mustang sales in the Chicago area soar off the charts.

Of all of the WLS DJs, Art Roberts, who had been working at WKBW in Buffalo, New York, was the most unlikely person to become a rock and roll disc jockey. Art was neither flashy nor "guffaw funny," but rather soft spoken, kind to a fault, a real student of music, and not just rock, but country, rhythm and blues, and folk. Art even understood the bizarre and what I considered to be the boring music styles of the day. These included such diverse artists as Bob Dylan, Patti Smith, Joni Mitchell, and Jimi Hendrix. Art taped a Sunday show in addition to his regular six-day week schedule in order to expose his audience to those different types of music. He called them "hooty, sapperticker nights," and Art and his audience not only had a ball but the listeners actually learned about different musical genres that weren't being heard normally on WLS.

Don Phillips came to the station from WRIT in Milwaukee and had, without a doubt, the toughest shift on the station: the all-night "East of Midnight Show." My hat goes off to anyone who clocks in from midnight to 5:30 A.M. When you work during that time slot, you sometimes feel like there isn't another person in the world listening to you. In reality, there were thousands of night owls in his radio audience. When you do that job, you are tired all the time and your health tends to suffer. But that didn't slow Don down a bit. He also had his own airplane, a 260 hp Navion, and he used it extensively for record hops, arriving back in Chicago at Meigs Field on the lakefront, jumping into a cab, and arriving in time to hit the airways at midnight. Don later went on to a very successful career as a stockbroker.

Steve King, who was on WLS from 1973 to 1978, and later worked with me at WIND, knows a thing or three about overnight shows. He went on to star on WGN-AM beginning in 1984, and he and his wife, Johnnie Putman, have done overnight shows for more than 20 years. They deserve a medal and more money because it truly is a topsy, turvy life.

The name Ray Van Steen wasn't well known to the WLS audience, yet he had a vital part in what went on the air. Ray was the production director who created all the wonderful contests and promotional ideas that were heard on the station. He was also the alter ego, "Peter Fugitive," who was heard on Art Robert's show.

The WLS Play List consisted of 60 to 65 songs each week. As record titles were dropped from the "Silver Dollar Survey," new ones were added. We also had what we called the "Local Playlist" which included Chicago garage bands that had demonstrated some promise. Some of those bands became huge national stars, such as the Buckinghams with *Kind of a Drag*, the Crying Shames with *Hey Baby*, the South Bend Rivieras with their West Coast sound on *California Sun*, the New Colony Six with Ronnie Rice on vocals, the Flock, and a great group, the One Eyed Jacks from Champaign, Illinois, who never had a national hit, but had a great sound. The Local Playlist not only put many local kids in the spotlight but it promoted the station to their fans, friends, and families, was one of the greatest promotions WLS ever had, and it didn't cost us a dime!

The program director is responsible for everything that goes on the air, including the music. The job also involves making sure that the station doesn't lose its license because of what is said or played on the air, and that included songs with suggestive lyrics. That was easy to do in the '50s and early '60s, but as we entered the mid '60s, some lyrics began to cross the line.

In fact, the strangest local group came about because of another group and an objectionable lyric. The Zombies were a British group that released a song with "hit" written all over it. However, one of the lyrics was, "I knocked on her bedroom door, and she let me in!" In the mid '60s, believe it or not, radio stations did a good job of policing such lyrics for two reasons: they didn't want to lose their FCC broadcasting license for playing objectionable songs; and, we programmers felt an obligation to keep the air waves clean. Today that sounds quaint, but it was very much on our minds in the '60s. While I was listening to the Zombies song, a Chicago record producer named Bill Trout came in to my office. I commented that the song was great, but I couldn't play it because the lyrics included the idea about a boy knocking on a girl's bedroom door and her letting him into her room. Trout asked, "Would you play that song if it didn't have that objectionable line in it?" I said, "sure," but I didn't give his comment another thought. The next morning, Bill was in my office with a test pressing of the revised record. He had been up all night rehearsing and recording the song with an unknown band. I put the new version on the WLS playlist, and the rest is history. The group was called the Shadows of Night and the million-seller was the song *Gloria*.

Another group, the Fuggs, had a song with the title of *Coca Cola Douche* that was easy to keep off the air. Then, there was Lou Christie who, in 1966, recorded a song called *Rhapsody in the Rain* for MGM and it included the lyric, "We were making out in the car when suddenly we went too far." Now, that is pretty tame today, but not the case in 1966. I wouldn't play the song on WLS, and Christie was irritated with my decision. I recall that he barged into my office and complained to me that there was nothing wrong with the lyric. I told him I was sorry but it was my decision, so Lou went back into the recording studios, re-recorded the song without that line, and it sold rather well.

In fact, I can only recall a few records that were either dumped by WLS or taken off the air. Two that come to mind were released in 1965: Barry McGuire's *Eve of Destruction*; and, a year later, Napoleon XIV with *They're Coming to Take Me Away*. Both records were initially aired, but because of many protests from listeners, we removed them from the WLS playlist. Many of the protests we received about *They're Coming to Take Me Away* were from mental health organizations which felt that the song was making fun of mental illness, while reactions to *Eve of Destruction* were concentrated on those who thought that the song was emphasizing anti-American attitudes about the Vietnam War.

I want to give a special "tip of the hat" to the WLS newsroom. While the newsmen and news writers weren't as glamorous as the disc jockeys, they were certainly an important part of the overall sound of the station. Some of the staff newsmen and announcers came over from the old WLS Prairie Farmer Station, including Jerry Golden, Jerry Mitchell, Bill Guthrie, and Stan Dale. By the mid 1960s, WLS expanded the news staff and suddenly the station took on a very well-schooled group of newsmen who wrote and reported their own news. Lyle Dean joined WLS from KOIL in Denver in 1968, and he reported the news until 1977. Lyle's voice was once described as so authoritative that if he said it was going to snow in July, you had better go out and buy tire chains. Lyle spent nine years at WLS, then on to WFYR before spending the next 24 years of his broadcasting career at WGN. He was a true Chicago news legend! Lyle and I remain best buddies to this day.

Mort Krim was also a part of the WLS Newsroom and went on to be the number one 10:00 P.M. news anchor on Detroit television for many years. In addition, those who worked at the station in the newsroom included Bob Benson, Bud Miller, Dick Harley, Jeff Henricks, and Chuck Scott. One of the news writers at that time, Jim Johnson, has remained at WLS to this day, spending over 40 years reporting the news for ABC and WLS.

RON RILEY'S BATMAN CLUB

The bearer of this card is an official member of the
Ron Riley Batman Club and is commissioned to assist
Batman and Robin in fighting the forces of evil.
Batman lives! POW!

Ron Riley
Ron Riley

Batman
Batman

WLS RADIO/WBKB-TV

left to right
Gene Taylor, Clark Weber, Ron Riley and Art Roberts at a benefit.

A certificate commissioning a listener as a "Lieutenant" in Weber's Commandos.

hEARYE

By all means, let this be known amongst ye:

That upon this day, His Imperialness, Emperor Weber of Weberland, Extinguished Candle that Lights the Way and Starts the Day, hath, by affixing His Imperial Marke, decreed, declared, demanded, and furthermore commissioned one:

_____

as

Lieutenant

of the Imperial Forces of Weberland, justly designated as Weber's Commandos, Guardians of the Empire!

Be it further known by these presents, that the Commissioned shall, as just reward for faithful following, share the fruitful bounty of Weberland, without interference, throughout the length and breadth of the Empire, as long as both ears shall listen!

Declared to be an
Imperial Signature upon
Imperial Paper by
His Imperialness

Chas Weber
Marke of His Imperialness

Nọ 21355

Printed in U.S.A.   WLS-1947-64

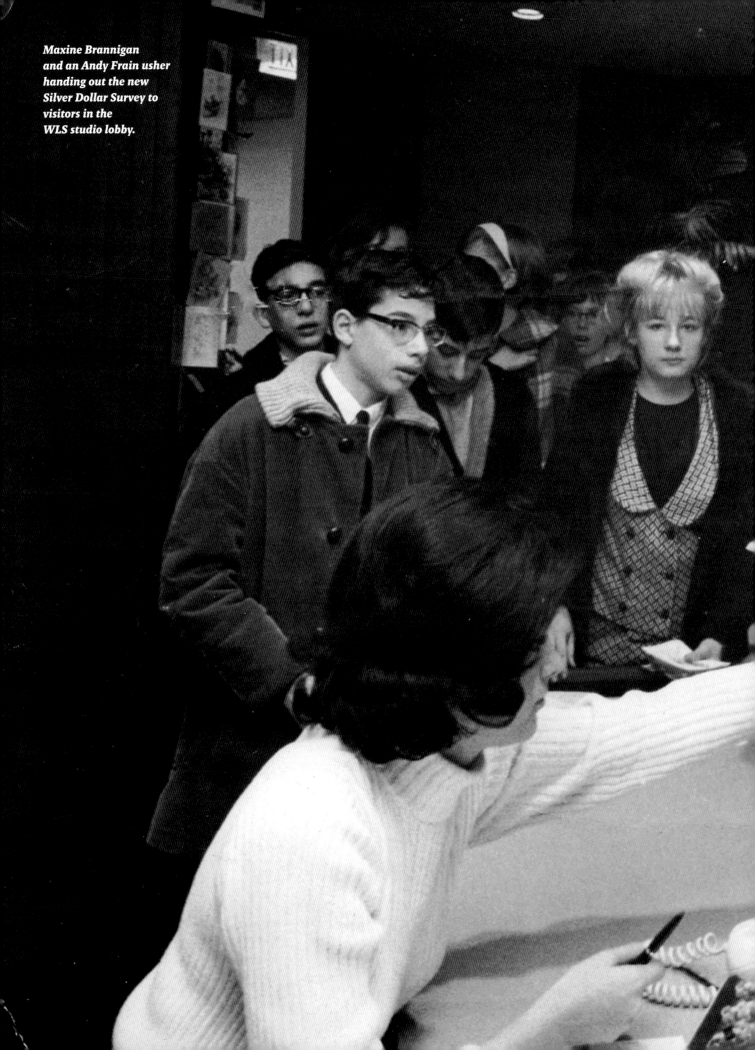

Maxine Brannigan and an Andy Frain usher handing out the new Silver Dollar Survey to visitors in the WLS studio lobby.

Two unknown fans who had won lunch with Clark Weber at the Brief Encounter restaurant on Michigan Avenue.

KEEP YOUR DIAL SET ON RADIO 890 AND HEAR
THE "NEW" BEATLES

CLARK
"BEATLE"
WEBER
6-9 AM

"RINGO"
TAYLOR
10-12 NOON

"BEATLE
BERNIE"
ALLEN
12:30 PM-
3:00 PM

"BOB
THE
BEATLE"
HALE
3:00-6:30 PM

"RINGO
RON"
RILEY
7:30-
9:00 PM

ART
"THE
EXCELSIOR
BEATLE"
ROBERTS
9:00-12 MIDNIGHT

DON
"BEATLE
ALL-NIGHT"
PHILLIPS
MIDNIGHT-
5:00 AM

WLS
The **bright** sound of Chicago Radio

SILVER BEATLE SURVEY

Chicago's Official Radio Record Survey

THIS WEEK	FEBRUARY 21, 1964		WEEKS PLAYED

* 1. I Want To Hold Your Hand .... The Beatles — Capitol 7
* 2. She Loves Me .... The Beatles — Swan 5
* 3. Dawn Go Away .... Four Seasons — Philips 7
* 4. Penetration .... The Pyramids — Best 7
* 5. Out Of Limits .... The Marketts — WB 7
* 6. See The Funny Little Clown .... Bobby Goldsboro — UA 9
* 7. Navy Blue .... Diane Renay — 20th Century 6
* 8. You Don't Own Me .... Lesley Gore — Mercury 10
* 9. A Letter From Sherry .... Dale Ward — Dot 9
*10. Hey Little Cobra .... The Ripchords — Columbia 10
 11. For You .... Rick Nelson — Decca 7
*12. Hi Heel Sneakers .... Tommy Tucker — Checker 6
*13. A Fool Never Learns .... Andy Williams — Columbia 9
*14. Java .... Al Hirt — RCA 13
*15. Fun Fun Fun .... The Beach Boys — Capitol 4
*16. California Sun .... The Rivieras — Riviera 13
*17. Stop And Think It Over .... Dale & Grace — Montel 7
*18. Please Please Me .... The Beatles — Vee Jay 2
*19. The Shelter Of Your Arms .... Sammy Davis Jr. — Reprise 3
*20. Abigail Beecher .... Freddie Cannon — WB 7
*21. I Love You More And More .... Al Martino — Capitol 7
*22. Um Um Um .... Major Lance — Okeh 7
*23. Rip Van Winkle .... The Devotions — Roulette 5
*24. Southtown U.S.A. .... The Dixiebelles — Sound Stage 7 7
 25. True Love Goes On And On .... Burl Ives — Decca 6
*26. Wow Wow Wee .... The Angels — Smash 7
*27. Glad All Over .... Dave Clark — Epic 6
*28. Bird Dance Beat .... The Trashmen — Garrett 5
*29. Bye Bye Barbara .... Johnny Mathis — Mercury 4
*30. I Saw Her Standing There .... The Beatles — Capitol 2
*31. It's All In The Game .... Cliff Richards — Epic 6
*32. Pink Dominoes .... The Crescents — Era 7
*33. Good News .... Sam Cooke — RCA 4
*34. Puppy Love .... Barbara Lewis — Atlantic 5
*35. Long Gone Lonesome Blues .... Hank Williams Jr. — MGM 4
*36. Think Nothing About It .... Gene Chandler — Constellation 4
*37. Vaya Con Dios .... The Drifters — Atlantic 4
*38. Little Boxes .... Pete Seeger — Columbia 3
*39. Shimmy Shimmy .... The Orlans — Cameo 3
*40. He Says The Same Things .... Skeeter Davis — RCA 4

FEATURED ALBUMS
THE GREAT HITS OF FRANK SINATRA — FRANK SINATRA — CAPITOL
THE SERENDIPITY SINGERS — PHILIPS

LISTEN TO
THE NEW
WLS BEATLES

WLS • DIAL 890 • 24 HOURS-A-DAY
ABC RADIO IN CHICAGO

This survey is compiled each week by WLS Radio/Chicago from reports of all
record sales gathered from leading record outlets in the Chicagoland area.
Hear Bob Hale play all the SILVER DOLLAR SURVEY hits daily from 3:00
to 6:30 P.M.   *Denotes record first heard in Chicago on WLS.

Almost all of the broadcast engineers came from the old WLS. They were part of the National Association of Broadcast Technicians Union, and you couldn't turn on a switch at the station until the engineers gave their okay. The DJ had no controls inside the studio and could only get his mike turned on by pointing to the microphone. A slash sign across the throat meant "kill the mike." If a DJ touched a microphone to move it around, the engineer could declare the studio "dead" for the next 24 hours until an engineer was brought in to move that piece of equipment. To put it mildly, that union was very protective of its membership. All records had to be recorded by an engineer, and the record had to be placed on the turntable, played by a member of the Musicians' Union, and then taped before the disc jockeys could play it on the air. It was an awkward system, but it worked. And, if that engineer became your "enemy," he could make life rough on you. Fortunately, the engineers were a happy lot. However, by the 1970s, the contracts of both the engineers and the musicians were bought out by ABC and, from then on, the DJs were able to operate the equipment in their studios.

Chapter 6
Behind The Scenes: The Sixties

After I had begun my career at WLS in the 1960s, several piano greats used to frequent WLS when its studios were in the London Guarantee Building at Michigan and Wacker, and not only rock stars, but the great jazz performers too. The London House nightclub was on the first floor of the building, and when the top stars wanted a break, they were invited to sit in the quiet of the WLS conference room and have a cup of coffee between sets. It was a "Who's Who" of jazz greats drinking our coffee– Jonah Jones, Errol Garner, Ramsey Lewis, and Oscar Peterson, just to name a few.

One night I was talking with Errol before I was supposed to go on my "East of Midnight" show. I remarked to him that it was ironic that he was at the London House playing wonderful jazz while, upstairs in the WLS studios, Dick Biondi was rocking away playing *Topsy Part 1 & 2*. Garner smiled, and said to me in his husky, cigarette-voice, "Man, its all music!"

Another piano star who frequently stopped at our station when he was in town was a good friend of WLS' general manager, Gene Taylor. Both Gene's friend and I would chide Taylor about his heavy smoking, but to no avail. The star had been a heavy smoker at one time, and probably as a result of his smoking, his African American complexion seemed to have already changed from polished ebony to ashen gray. Gene would later die of emphysema, but not before his friend, the great piano player and singer with a soft voice, had died from lung cancer. That popular performer, who sold millions of records and had his own television show, was Nat King Cole.

While Mother Weber may have taught me how to dress, and my wife, Joan, on more than one occasion has said to me, "You're not going out dressed like that," it took the late, great Bob Hope to shape up my onstage image. Bob was doing a show at the Condessa Del Mar Club on Cicero Avenue in Alsip. It was his first nightclub appearance in 40 years, and I was the emcee. Before the show, Bob complimented me on the suit I was wearing. I thanked him, since I have always wanted to look sharp at personal appearances. However, Bob followed his compliment by saying, "But, I could never wear that suit on stage." After taking a quick look at Bob's suit, I replied, "Why on earth not?" Although his suit was well-tailored, it was far from sharp and seemed to me to be even a little dull looking. His answer was brilliant. He said, "The guy in the audience, the guy who was in World War II or at one of my USO shows in Korea or Vietnam remembers me wearing either GI clothes or a golf shirt. A sharp suit would get in the way of his memory, and it would make me look too elite."

Before the evening was over, Hope also taught me a second lesson. After his show, a woman approached and asked if her husband could take a picture of the three of us. We said yes, of course, and she stood between us and asked if we would put our arms around her shoulders. Bob told her no and said to me that after her husband took the picture he would explain. It seems that many years ago he agreed to a picture standing next to a fan with his arm around her shoulder. When his wife, Doris, saw the photo, she pointed out that when he did that the lapels on his suit spread out and looked like a pair of wings. Thanks for the memories Bob, and the lessons on how to dress!

As I look back on that decade I realize that there were several business deals that came my way during the 1960s, some of which I was forced to reject, others that didn't happen but worked out in my favor. One potential deal was related to an air freight line that flew mail between Las Vegas and Los Angeles. It turned out to be a good thing that I rejected the offer to invest in it because three of the freight line planes crashed and the company went bankrupt.

However, there were other potential deals that would have seriously changed my financial future and those rejections haunt me to this day. Gene Taylor, Harvey Wittenberg, the manager of WLS-FM, and I were approached to buy an FM radio station that was located across the street from WLS. The station had gone bankrupt and was available to be purchased for only $30,000. After checking our ABC contracts, we discovered that we were legally forbidden from owning a competing radio or television station.

But, the deal that still wakes me up in the middle of the night concerned a single record and the little company that created it. One day in the '60s, the owner of that record flew into Chicago, visited me at WLS, and asked me to listen to a demo copy of a song he had written

*Bob Hope and Clark Weber
at an appearance.*

and produced. I thought that the song was so different from anything I had heard that I felt it could possibly be a hit record. He became very excited because I was the first deejay DJ who told him that it had potential for success. Everyone else had said that it was too weird and, besides, it had a foreign sound to it. After giving him my positive reaction, the owner of the record asked me if I was interested in buying a third of his company along with the record. It seemed that the guy and his partner had recorded the song in a studio in their garage, but they had no money to begin promoting it. So, he offered me a 1/3 ownership for only $9,000. I told him that I would think it over that night and get back to him the next day.

That evening, Joan took out my ABC/WLS contract and read me the provision that forbade my having any ownership in a record company. So, I had to reluctantly tell him "thanks, but no thanks." To put it mildly, the record became a big hit and the owners became rather rich. The record was *The Lonely Bull* and it was performed by Herb Alpert and the Tijuana Brass. Herb and his partner, Jerry Moss, sold A&M (Alpert and Moss) Records in 1989 for $500 million. Let's see...a 1/3 of that would be $166 million.

One of the greatest stars whose career began in the '60s was Diane Ross (she later changed her name to Diana) and the Supremes. In 1965, Motown released *Stop In the Name of Love* which was followed with the Supremes' hit *Come See About Me*. Florence Ballard was a fun lady who sang lead on many of their earlier songs, while Mary Wilson was a sweet person who appeared to be unaffected by any possible friction between Ballard and Ross. Flo was the one who got the group its initial audition with Berry Gordy, the owner of Detroit's Motown Records, and a very successful singing career followed for the group.

It is my sense that, over the years, a lot of record producers often took unfair advantage of their artists. But Gordy was not one of those producers. First, he insisted that the members of the Supremes finish high school. Then, once they became budding stars, he sent them to charm school where they were taught how to stand (note Diana's hand on her hip in the adjoining photograph), how to dress, how to behave on stage, and how to deal with the media. In the early '60s, the group worked well as a team, but, in 1967, Ballard apparently felt that she was being pushed out by Ross and decided to quit the group.

The demands on the trio, including a heavy traveling schedule and a quick rise to stardom, began to cause problems. Allegedly, Diana was not the easiest person with whom to work, and when Florence quit, Cindy Birdsong was brought in as her replacement on the Supremes. Sadly, Flo eventually ended up on welfare and died of a heart attack in 1976, and by the early '70s, the Supremes had broken up. However, Diana Ross continued to record and tour as a single and became a major recording star.

One of the most unfortunate stories from those years related to the very popular singer Bobby Darin. Darin was always gracious as he climbed up the "rock and roll ladder." From *Splish Splash* in the '50s to *Having Your Baby* in the '60s, Bobby was a class act, although he was sometimes known to be a bit brash. As I understand it, Darin once bragged to Frank Sinatra that he was going to be a bigger star than Frank ever hoped to be. Needless to say, that claim did not make Sinatra very happy. Nonetheless, the hits continued to come Bobby's way as did Las Vegas nightclub appearances, movies, and Darin's marriage to Sandra Dee. However, their wedded bliss lasted only a few years until 1967, and by that time, his career was not going well. He was divorced, reportedly experiencing serious financial problems, and living in a tiny trailer in Los Angeles.

In 1968, I was booked to emcee a rock concert at the National Guard Armory in South Bend, Indiana. On the bill were the local rock band, the Rivieras, ready to play their big national hit, *California Sun*, Peter, Paul and Mary, and Bobby Darin. When I arrived at the armory, I was met by Mary Travers who said, "Clark, Bobby wants to change the way you introduce him to the crowd."

As I walked into Darin's dressing room, I was surprised, to put it mildly. Although Bobby always prided himself on his hairpiece, which looked quite real, that day he was as bald as me. He stood there with his hairpiece in his hand and announced that he was going to appear on stage au natural without the piece. Furthermore, he informed me that he was to be introduced as "Bob Darin" and not Bobby. He requested a chair be placed in the middle of the stage as his only prop. Boy, this was getting weird! The armory was packed, and the Rivieras opened the show. They were great, as usual, and then it was time for Darin to perform. I introduced him to a huge round of applause, and out onto the stage walked Bobby Darin with his guitar. The audience was stunned because they had come to the concert expecting to see this cocky, great rock and roll legend. Instead, they saw a bald headed guy with a mustache, shabbily dressed, and seeming to be mumbling his welcome to the crowd. His opening number was an original song I had never heard before about the late Bobby Kennedy. It seems that Darin had been a part of Kennedy's campaign in 1968 before he was assassinated. It was a real downer for an opening song at a rock and roll concert. He followed that with a Vietnam protest song, and the audience responded by sitting on its hands. They just couldn't figure him out.

Meanwhile, I was standing in the wings trying to loudly whisper to Darin, "You're dying out there. You had better rock!" Finally, something in the back of his mind caused him to realize the audience's negative reaction and he began to pick up the pace by performing his hit songs *Splish Splash, Mack the Knife*, and *Up a Lazy River*. Mercifully, it was a short set and as he walked off the stage, the South Bend audience was too polite to boo his performance. Yet, they had every right to react that way. I immediately introduced Peter, Paul and Mary, and they tore the place up. While I walked back to the dressing room with Darin, he asked me how he had done. I said to him, "Bob, this audience doesn't give a rat's ass about your political beliefs. They came to the concert to hear you entertain, and you just barely did that!" The following year, Darin attempted to jump-start his career once again in Vegas, but was only greeted with fair reviews. Sadly, Bobby Darin died on the operating table in 1973 while doctors were attempting to replace a defective heart valve. It has always remained true in the world of entertainment that the public generally doesn't care about the political viewpoints of performing artists. Sometimes it even leads to boycotts against such performers.

Two of my favorite people from the rock and roll years who are still performing today are Steve Lawrence and his wife Edie Gorme. They were able to withstand the need to make rock and roll records in the '60s and yet sell a lot of their singles and albums like *Go Away Little Girl* and *Blame It On The Bossa Nova*. To this day, they still get large audiences for their concerts around the country. In the mid-'60s, they were booked to play Chicago, and Joan and I, along with Don Phillips and his wife Doris, were invited to a Columbia Records cocktail party to welcome them back to town. I had known Steve and Edie for several years, as well as Steve's brother Bernie. Bernie qualifies as an even more devious practical joker than me. On the night of this classy cocktail party, Bernie took me aside, pointed out a particular waiter, and told me to just watch the guy without explaining what was going to happen. I thought that there was nothing different about the guy than the several other waiters who

"As a rock and roll deejay, I reluctantly found myself in situations where I observed the top performers of the '50s and '60s sometimes reaching stardom and then having spats over a wide variety of issues."

"As can be imagined, many recording stars could get on each others' nerves in the course of being on the road together for too many days and doing shows night after night."

Mark Weber,
...iane (before she...
...the Supremes.

Steve Lawrence, Don Phillips and Edie Gorme.

Edie Gorme and Clark Weber.

were working at the party. Then, all of a sudden, that waiter put down his drink tray, walked up to Edie with paper and pencil in hand and asked for her autograph. She had just finished signing the paper when all hell broke loose. The waiter looked at her autograph and exclaimed in a loud voice— "Oh my gosh, you're Edie Gorme!"—and proceeded to leap what seemed like five feet in the air, do a back flip and land flat on his back on the carpet. Edie was absolutely stunned, turned ashen, and rushed over to the guy assuming that he was hurt. She immediately asked him if he was all right, and his response was to open his eyes, stand up, and do another flip after yelling out, "Edie Gorme!" Bernie and I were doubled over in laughter, and when she recovered, Edie said to us, "I might have known one of you would be behind this stunt!"

Another famous singing duo was Sonny and Cher. Sonny had been a 29-year-old record promoter when he met the 16-year-old Cher, took her by the musical hand, and guided her into a singing career. At that time, Cher's musical credits consisted of being a backup singer for the Ronettes on their hit record, *Be My Baby*. When she was just 19, Sonny and Cher got married.

By 1967, the success of their records had stalled. Their hit singles, including *I Got You Babe* and *The Beat Goes On,* were behind them and they needed another hit song. After the Beatles had become so successful with their songs and movies, the Dave Clark Five and the Monkees made money for their groups by also making movies. So, Sonny hired producer, and former Chicagoan, William Friedkin, to produce a movie for him and Cher called *Good Times,* which Sonny and Cher's young fans just loved. The film company that had made the movie contacted me and asked me to join Sonny and Cher for a whirlwind opening tour of the movie in Chicago where I would be the emcee at 20 theaters over a two-day time period. It seemed like a piece of cake, but, as I remember it, at that time, Cher was upset with the IRS, Sonny, and anyone who came within earshot of her.

During the two days of the tour, Cher spent much time sitting in the back of the bus and anyone who came near her could see that she was angry. When I asked Sonny about the situation, he told me that she was upset with him over the movie (which she hadn't wanted to do), the fact that they owed $200,000 in back taxes to the IRS, and that their records weren't selling.

To her credit, Cher did put on a happy face at each of our appearances during the promotional tour of the movie theaters, and then it was back on the bus. Ironically, neither Sonny nor Cher knew at the time that the movie had caught the eye of some television executives who were impressed with the special chemistry between the two of them. Eventually, they would go on to star on their very popular *Sonny and Cher Comedy Hour* on CBS-TV.

As a rock and roll DJ, I reluctantly found myself in situations where I observed the top performers of the '50s and '60s sometimes reaching stardom and then having spats over a wide variety of issues. I remember one morning when I had a breakfast meeting with Paul Simon and Art Garfunkel, friends since sixth grade. We got together right after my morning show at the Executive House, on Wacker Drive, just around the corner from the WLS studios. I no sooner pulled up a chair when I could sense they were upset with each other for no particular reason. The combination of being on the road for long periods of time combined with artistic differences concerning their music, and whatever else was going on, made for a long breakfast that morning. Years later, I read in the music trade papers that they broke up the duo once again and then reformed it when their individual careers stalled. Go figure!

Sonny and Cher with Art Roberts at the WLS studios.

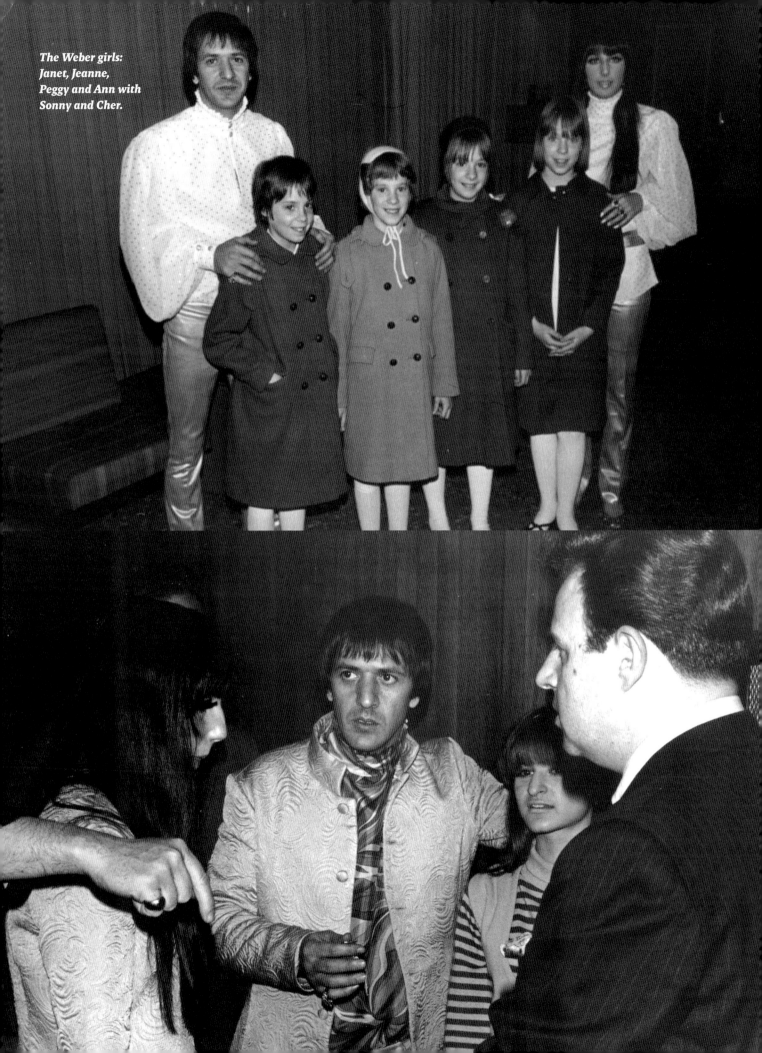

The Weber girls: Janet, Jeanne, Peggy and Ann with Sonny and Cher.

One of my favorite stories happened during the '60s when there was a group created and packaged by a major record company with a cute look, a hit record, a so-so movie, and a television show. In other words, they were making money. They decided to pay a visit to WLS and say hello as a goodwill gesture to help support their career. Someone had told them to act a little crazy and create some attention, and when they arrived in our lobby they seemed to go nuts.

One of them actually began climbing up our expensive drapes, and halfway up, the drapes tore, the rods ripped out of the wall, and all of it tumbled down. I saw the mess, and my reaction was to throw the four goofy rock and rollers out of WLS. RCA records heard about what happened and were appalled. The record company assured me that they would pay for the damages and that the group would apologize to us. Sure enough, the next day, one member of the group, withcap in hand, visited me at the station, said that all four of them were sorry for what had happened, and I decided to accept the apology. The singing group climbing our drapes and in essence, trying to catch *The Last Train to Clarksville*, were none other than The Monkees.

Another adventure happened in 1965 when a movie escort job got me into trouble. Singer and actress Connie Stevens had been paired with Dean Jones and Cesar Romero in a campy little movie called *Two on a Guillotine*. In the movie's final scene, Connie's head was made to look as if it had been cut off on a chopping block as the guillotine's blade came down on her neck—and then the movie ended. The publicity stunt I was asked to perform was to walk onto the stage carrying a lifelike "head" of Connie Stevens, complete with curly blond hair. The fake head had been created by the studio's wardrobe department and the idea was to freak out the kids in the audience. I was supposed to give a small talk about the scene and then introduce the charming, and very alive, Connie Stevens.

We were doing this stunt in 20 theatres all over Chicago during a two-day period. On one of those afternoons, Connie and I arrived at a movie theater a little early, just before the final scene in the film. We stood behind the last row of the darkened movie theater in order to watch the kids react. As the movie reached its climax, I noticed a teenage girl who was really caught up in the movie. She was very frightened, squirming in her seat and yelling, "No! No!" Just as the guillotine fell on Connie's head in the film, I reached over and dropped Connie's lifelike head into this teenage girl's lap. I don't know what I expected to happen, but the kid lost it! Connie's fake head was in her lap, she was screaming bloody murder, and she even lost control of her bladder. Then, the houselights came on and Connie rushed over, put her arms around the girl, and tried to calm her down. While that was a kind gesture on Connie's part, the girl had just the opposite reaction. She looked at Connie and became so star struck with the idea that Connie Stevens was holding her that she burst into tears. Of course, I was the bad guy in the event, and I quickly apologized to the girl for what I had done. Connie also scolded me, but she later admitted that it was hilarious.

As can be imagined, many recording stars could get on each others' nerves in the course of being on the road together for too many days and doing shows night after night. I recall having to referee a dispute between two singers named Paul & Paula. They were best known for their hit song, *Hey, Hey Paula*, in the mid-'60s. Some stage door chick was attracted to Paul, and Paula became so upset one night that I thought she was going hit Paul. That night, they came on from opposite sides of the stage and glared at each other while they sang love songs to each other.

*Clark Weber
holding Connie Stevens'
"head."*

Connie greeting the audience at the opening of her movie, Two For The Guillotine.

The Monkees' Mickey Dolenz and Peter Tork apologize for tearing the drapes off the wall in the WLS lobby.

Dave Clark,
Public Relations man Jim Feely,
and Clark Weber.

A photo in the WLS magazine that features Dave Clark, Clark Weber, Mary Beth Weber, Clark's sister, and a friend, Mary McCleneghan.

But the most bizarre spat I ever witnessed went on for 13 years on stage, and perhaps you never knew it. It was in the late '60s when I emceed a live show at the Chicago Amphitheatre. Before going on stage, I had to be briefed about the star act. The headliners were two guys who had a couple of monster hits and, yet, refused to speak to each other. I don't just mean on stage, I mean at all! It seems that singer A had shot his wife in the face during a domestic dispute. She survived, but singer B was so incensed over the incident that he refused to speak to singer A ever again...and he didn't. For 13 years following that incident, night after night, these two guys electrified audiences around the country with their great stage act, complete with back and forth singing, microphone and jacket tossing, and stunning foot work, to say nothing of making hit records. That night at the Amphitheatre, the crowd was on its feet and just going crazy! Yet, when their shows were over, these two talented singers went their separate ways and never spoke to each other again. One later died in an auto accident and the other, allegedly, of a drug overdose. Even today their songs get people dancing, including such great hits as *Hold On, I'm Comin'* and *Soul Man*. You knew these guys as Sam Moore and Dave Prather, and, years later, Jake and Elwood, in the movie *The Blues Brothers*, did their version of *Soul Man*, and it was a hit all over again!

In the mid-1960s, a popular British rock group, the Dave Clark Five, burst onto the record scene and their record, *Glad All Over* quickly climbed to number six on the WLS Silver Dollar Survey. Soon after, they released a movie called *Having A Wild Weekend,* and it was scheduled to open in Chicago on the weekend of August 13-14, 1965. Several months earlier, I announced on WLS my prediction that the Dave Clark Five would become even bigger and better than the Beatles. My comment not only irritated the teen audience listening to my "arch rival" Ron Riley, but it was also received by many as blasphemy and they howled at my comparison. However, Dave Clark's banging drum in *Glad All Over* helped that record to become very popular. The motion picture company producing the movie decided to hire me to accompany the DC5 to 18 Chicago-area movie theaters for two days to introduce the group to the packed houses of kids. The band did a short set of their hits, and the kids went crazy. In fact, one kid crossed an acceptable line of behavior when he lit a cigarette lighter, held it with a pair of pliers until it was red hot, and then threw it at the Dave Clark Five while they were on stage. The lighter struck the late singer Mike Smith in the head and scarred him for life. Although we didn't catch the jerk who threw the lighter, it pointed out that there is always the chance for a twisted mind to be a part of every crowd. Meanwhile, the battle for record supremacy continued for awhile.

Then, of course, there were the Beatles. In 1964, the success of the Beatles' *Hard Day's Night,* which had been inexpensive to produce, didn't escape the notice of executives in the record industry. It appeared to be a way to sell more records and anything else that the adoring young public would buy! In 1965, I innocently somehow got into a squabble with George Harrison of the Beatles.

It all started back when Vee-Jay Records released the Beatles' first record, *Please, Please Me,* and the flip side, *Ask Me Why*. WLS had been "burned" a few months earlier by another British rock star named Cliff Richard, whose record went nowhere in the U.S., and we were very leery of promoting another British rock group. Yet, more as a favor to the owners of Vee-Jay, Vivian Carter and James Bracken, we took a shot at it. Dick Biondi was the first WLS DJ to get the go ahead to begin playing the Beatles record. It turns out that it was no honor! I'll be gracious and simply say that, in my opinion, the record did not meet my standards of excellence.

We played it for two weeks, took it off the air, and then put it back on again for another two weeks, thanks to the pleading of Vee-Jay along with the Beatles growing popularity in England. Finally, the song was killed and meanwhile Vee-Jay entered into a legal battle with Capitol Records over the rights to the group. Capitol prevailed, and, in later years, Vee-Jay admitted that if they had won that battle, it would have sunk their company since the demand for the Beatles' songs was such that the record company couldn't financially handle it. When Capitol re-released the Beatles material, it was under the direction of producer George Martin and didn't sound anything like the Beatles of old. Capitol had to make the case to WLS and other major radio stations in the U.S. that the group was worthy of a second chance, and they launched a major press, print, and promotional push to get the stations onboard—and it worked.

By 1965, Capitol decided on a Beatles' nationwide concert tour, including Chicago. To honor the four moptops, Capitol held a luncheon on August 20, 1965 for the WLS DJs and the Beatles at the Saddle and Cycle Club on North Lake Shore Drive. An old public relations friend of mine, Jim Feely, was dating a tall and lovely blonde model named Edwina Rast, AKA "Winky the Weather Bunny," who worked on WLS. He wondered if I could get Winky into the party to meet the Beatles. I said, "sure," and arranged for her to attend. She showed up in a two-piece tennis outfit, and I seated her next to George Harrison who took one look at this blonde arm candy and somehow figured that she was his door prize. After about 20 minutes of conversation, Winky stood up, thanked Harrison, and announced that she had to leave for a modeling audition. Harrison said, "You can't go," but Winky's reply was, "Watch me!" and left.

George told me that he was furious with me for allowing her to leave. "Not true," I told him, "I had nothing to do with her decision to leave." To deflect his unhappiness, I shifted my attention to music conversations with McCartney, Starr, and Lennon. Meanwhile, their manager, Brian Epstein was running around trying to keep a lid on these kids. Overall, they reminded me of four youngsters from Hammond or Gary who had struck it big but were overwhelmed by their new found fame.

Later that afternoon, my friend Jim Feely called again, said that Winky had a wonderful time meeting the Beatles, and wondered if I could get her into the concert scheduled that night at Comiskey Park. It was a sold-out show with over 33,000 screaming kids shelling out $4.50 to see the Beatles. I commented that Feely was pushing our friendship, but, yeah, I would get her into the concert. Winky showed up in a skintight black cocktail dress and stood alongside me right next to the stage to watch the Beatles. I say "watch" because you couldn't hear them even up close. DJs Bernie Allen, Dex Card, and I stepped onto the stage to introduce the Beatles, and we could feel the sound of those thousands of screaming kids through our fingers. When the Beatles came out on stage, we never heard a single note during their 45-minute show. Later, that was one of the reasons why the group quit touring nationally—no one could hear them.

Twenty-five years later I received a call from a *Chicago Sun-Times* photographer who was retiring to Las Vegas and cleaning out his photo files. He told me that he had a photograph which he wanted to send to me. When I opened up the envelope, there was a photo of the Beatles on stage at Comiskey Park while, off stage I was standing there just looking bored with my hands on my hips because I couldn't hear anything. Standing next to me was Winky, and when you looked at George Harrison, you could see him giving this beautiful, leggy blonde the eye.

left to right
Clark Weber, Edwina "Winky" Rast, Dex Card, and The Beatles at Comiskey Park in Chicago.

Chapter 7
Not All Stars Shine at First

People fail in direct proportion to their willingness to accept socially acceptable excuses for failure. In show business, far more people fail than make it. The ones who succeed do so because of timing, talent, and pure luck. There are also some who simply don't know the meaning of the word "quit."

As the Program Director of WLS in the mid '60s, I met them all. One day in 1963, I had a call from Columbia record promoter Freddie Salem, who had a problem and needed a favor. It seems that Columbia had signed a relatively unknown singer to an album contract. She had just finished an appearance at Bon Soir, a small New York club, and based on that performance was booked at Mister Kelly's on Chicago's Rush Street. It was the early part of her career, and she may not have been well known to many Chicagoans. Consequently, she was drawing relatively small crowds to the club, and as could be expected, she was less than happy with the situation. I was told that the singer felt that there had been a lack of publicity about her appearances. Salem asked that Joan and I join him for dinner at Mister Kelly's so that we could hear her sing and also to help fill up the place.

I should note that show business is not my wife's favorite thing, but, being a good sport, we showed up together for the Friday night show. It was a good thing we did because the place was almost empty. The singer, who would go on to be a superstar in her nightclub, recording, and acting career, definitely showed promise but, at that time, it was my judgment that she would need to improve her singing voice in order to become a star. Well that turned out to be an understatement. After the set was over, she joined us at our table to make small talk. She was complaining about the fact that the piano squeaked, her accommodations in Chicago were less than adequate, and Columbia Records was just not treating her well. Then, Joan, in an effort to get the young lady to focus on more positive issues, changed the subject and asked about the singer's hometown and her family. It soon became abundantly clear to us that the 22-year-old wasn't close to her family and didn't really care if anyone knew it. I looked at Salem, and he rolled his eyes in dismay. After the singer left to get ready for her next set, Joan announced that it was time for us to go home.

The following Monday, on a hot July day, Salem showed up at my WLS office with this singer in tow to present me with a copy of her first album. She was dressed in a style that I would describe as right out of the late '60s: short skirt, purple tights, thigh high black boots, full cape and deer stalker hat. None of the outfit seemed to match, but despite all initial appearances, she became, by far, one of the most popular singers of her generation and recently earned $95 million in record sales and appearances in one year. Her name—Barbra Streisand!

In 1966, a 25-year-old New York music composer and performer convinced Bang Records to produce a couple of his songs and then send him out on the road to visit radio stations. The idea was to team him up with a local record promotion man and get some air play. The problem was that nobody had ever heard of this guy, he had no musical track record, and, as a result, he experienced rejections at a variety of places. The other difficulty was that, in 1966, the country was awash in established rock and roll hits by such big stars as The Beatles, The Mommas and The Poppas, and The Monkees, just to name a few.

Kent Beauchamp of Royal Disc Distributors in Chicago called on me one day, and in the course of pitching records he asked me listen to this New York singer's recording. Beauchamp, an old friend of mine, admitted that no one in the country was playing the song, but Kent still wanted me to hear it. I listened, played it again, and thought that, just maybe, the singer might have something. I played it a third time and decided to put the record on the WLS "Playlist" for a two-week, trial basis. Beauchamp was delightfully surprised and mentioned that the artist was with him that day, although not in the building. I said, "Where is he?" Kent told me that the guy was so afraid of rejection that he was waiting outside our studios, on the corner of Michigan Avenue and Wacker Drive in front of the London House, just anticipating another negative reaction to his song. I told Kent to bring the singer up to my office and, when he came into the station, I informed him that WLS had decided to play the song. He was very excited at the good news, and the record turned out to be the first of many huge hits for the singer/composer whom WLS gave his first big break. That song was *Solitary Man*, and the guy who was afraid to hear the verdict was none other than Neil Diamond.

I'm the first to admit that I didn't always hear "hit record" when a song was first played. In 1965, I was doing a beach party record hop at the Glen Lord Beach park pavilion in Niles, Michigan when a very polite teenager asked me if I would listen to a record that he and his friends had written and recorded. I said that I would and put it on the turntable. My first reaction was that it was a bit primitive, but I decided to be gentle in my response. I told him that while it was a good first try, it wasn't something that WLS would have an interest in playing on the air. Yet, soon after, a Pittsburgh DJ started playing the song, and in a while it took off. Before you knew it, Roulette Records heard it and signed the singer to a contract in 1966. It became such a big hit that people still dance to it today. The kid's name was Tommy James, and the song was *Hanky Panky*.

There is no one prouder of a child's talent than a parent. I had a call from a Gary, Indiana steelworker concerning a song his kids had recorded. It was starting to get the attention of teenagers across Chicago's South Side. In 1966, there were still two worlds of music: rock and roll and rhythm and blues. While WLS was, at that time, playing groups like the Temptations, Diana Ross and the Supremes, the Drifters, and Sam Cooke, the hard R&B, as it was called, hadn't crossed over into the world of the white record buyers. On two occasions, WLS featured R&B weekends at which time we played hard core rhythm and blues music. Yet, on both occasions, the experiment seemed to fail. The white kids still weren't buying hard-edged R&B songs recorded by black artists, and the same was true for black teenagers when it came to white singers. They each seemed to have their own musical worlds and specific tastes in music.

However, the father from Gary was undeterred and asked if he could bring his kids to my office. I said "Sure!", and the kids not only showed up, but they brought their musical instruments with them, set them up right there in my office, and began playing their song. While it was strictly what I classified as "soul bubblegum," I thought that it wasn't bad. The lead singer of the group was only eight years old, and he moved around like a puppet on a string. When WLS didn't play the group's first record, the father was unhappy with us. The group later signed with Motown Records in Detroit, and we got on board with their next, and improved, second record several months later. The proud father was Joe Jackson, his kids were called The Jackson Five, and little Michael "fronted" the group.

One of the most bizarre people I ever met during my years as a DJ was a New York record producer who occasionally came to my office at WLS with his record promotion man, Danny Davis. When I knew him, that producer was a bright and seemingly arrogant 21-year-old who had an incredible string of hit records under his belt. The fact that he knew his craft well was defined by the fact that he had produced several million-selling records. Some of the relative unknowns who were under his guidance included the Teddy Bears, the Crystals, the Ronnettes, and the Righteous Brothers.

This producer would add an echo effect to many of his records and then dub and redub over the lyric lines. Suddenly the music world took notice of him. At that time, he couldn't

"As record hops in the '60s increased in number and popularity in and around Chicago, and became big money makers for various church organizations, they found that as time went on they had to add big name rock bands to attract the teenagers."

"If there is one thing worse than failure in show business it is rising to the top too quickly and not being able to handle the fame. On the other hand, if that success builds slowly, you can usually keep your perspective and not lose sight of who, and what, you are."

Clark Weber signing autographs at one of hundreds of record hops during the 1960s.

have weighed more than 120 pounds soaking wet and had a hairdo that looked like he had backed into an electric wall socket. He wore the latest British footwear called "Fruit Boots" with pointed toes and lifts to give him the appearance of being much taller, and he could hardly sit still. We would talk about the world of hit music and the direction of music trends as he continually moved around the room. But that wasn't the creepy part. He wore a holstered snub nose .38-caliber revolver on his right hip and didn't make any effort to conceal it. He told me he carried the gun because, as part of his work, he often traveled in what he considered a lot of dangerous neighborhoods while auditioning singers. He said that he wanted the gun for protection. I grew up with firearms since my dad was a detective on the Milwaukee County Sheriff's Department, but there was something about this record producer and the love affair he had for his weapon that unsettled me. Years later, this guy has had more than his fair share of trouble because of guns. His name: Phil Spector.

As record hops in the '60s increased in number and popularity in and around Chicago, and became big money makers for various church organizations, they found that as time went on they had to add big name rock bands to attract the teenagers. Paul Revere and the Raiders certainly were a draw and with a couple of hits under their belts, including *Indian Reservation* and later, *Kicks*, they wowed the teenagers. Brother Rice High School on South Pulaski Road in Chicago decided to throw a big hop and booked the Raiders. They also hired me to emcee the party. The place was packed to the rafters with kids, including hundreds of girls who had teenage crushes on Mark Lindsay, the good looking vocalist for the Raiders. Midway through the dance, the band was rocking and Lindsay was doing a song that was almost drowned out by the screams of the girls. To further stir up the young ladies, Lindsay took the microphone and lay down on the stage floor, all the while continuing to sing.

The girls went absolutely crazy, and that was when Mark made one mistake. He was lying down too close to the edge of the stage within arms reach of the audience. An overly enthusiastic female fan reached up towards the prone Mr. Lindsay, grabbed him by his "manhood," and held on for dear life. Lindsay's voice went from singing to screaming because the girl wouldn't let go. Several Brother Rice priests rushed the stage and attempted to pry the girl's fingers from around Mr. Lindsay's "pride and joy." Well, no dice, because she had her grab bag prize and wanted to take it home. I was laughing so hard I began crying while the band started playing *Hold That Tiger*, and Mark saw his future flash before his eyes. Finally, after a tug of war, the priests prevailed, the girl gave up, and to this day, Lindsay claims that there are fingerprints on his genitalia and that his voice has remained at least half an octave higher.

Early in my career, my Uncle Hank, a wise old farmer, recognized long before I did that maybe I was going to make it in show business. He gave me the following good advice: "Clark, someday someone is going to call you a star. It's okay to taste fame, but don't swallow it!" If there is one thing worse than failure in show business it is rising to the top too quickly and not being able to handle the fame. On the other hand, if that success builds slowly, you can usually keep your perspective and not lose sight of who, and what, you are.

One Monday morning in August 1966, I had a call from a record promoter who told me about an act that was booked into a North Avenue club. However, they only lasted there a few weeks before being fired. The club owner refused to pay them because he felt that they were driving his customers away and told them to get out of the club before he threw them out. They made the decision to show up at WLS, seek me out, and tell me their sad story of being broke, scared, and hungry. In general, they looked to me like deer caught in headlights.

They attacked our coffee pot as if they were people possessed while the group's vocalist sat in my office and told me their tale of woe. She said that they were from the West Coast and had no way to get back home. The young lady was a mess and she looked and smelled as if she had lived in her clothes for at least a day or two. Then, she asked if she could use my office phone to call a friend in San Francisco, and I told her to "be my guest." However, once she got her friend on the phone they began to argue. It seems that he was willing to pay for the group's airfare back to California only if she and the band agreed to record several songs for him. She later told me that she didn't like his music but had no choice except to agree to his demand.

Back they went to 'Frisco where they did indeed record for him. But, little came of the songs, although she would soon have a string of hit singles and albums. Then, in October 1970, that singer recorded a song that did become a hit. That's the good news. The bad news is that success came so fast that within four months of the song rising in the charts, she was dead from drugs and alcohol. The hit song that was part of her third album, and sold posthumously, was an old Kris Kristoferson song called *Me and Bobby McGee*, and, of course, the singer was Janis Joplin.

Disk Jockeys Mass for TV Show

A LIVELY exchange of ideas is expected when the entire disk jockey staff of WLS radio makes a special television appearance on Kumzitz, Sunday at 11 a. m., on channel 7.

Appearing with Clark Weber, Bernie Allen, Dex Card, Ron Riley, Art Roberts, and Don Phillips from WLS, will be Lois Brooks as moderator and a record-breaking (in size at least) audience of teen-agers. An added attraction will be the appearance of ABC - Paramount recording aritsts, The Kittens.

Under discussion during the program will be the lofty subject of "Morality—1965."

Ron Bailey of the Tribune's color studio, assembled and photographed the group shown on this page.

Created by Henry Mamet of the Chicago Board of Rabbis, Kumzitz is a careful blending of popular elements

TV's Lois Brooks with the six radio disk jockeys who will appear on her program Sunday. Clockwise: Clark Weber, Dex Card, Bernie Allen, Art Roberts, and Ron Riley.

of entertainment with thought-provoking ideas.

According to Mamet, also producer of the show, the word Kumzitz is an old-world expression that means "come and sit." It was an old custom to gather at someone's home and sit and talk or sing.

The setting of the show has captured the idea with a modern setting, a corner ice cream parlor where the youngsters come to dance their crazy new steps and listen to the music of the juke box.

Mixed in with the fun and song is the introduction of a subject of current interest to stimulate conversation among the young set.

Topics have ranged from sex education to civil rights demonstrations, and in recognition of the contribution the show makes, this year the series received the Board of Governors award of the Academy of Television Arts and Sciences.

They'll Tackle the Problem of "Morality—1965"

One of "Emperor" Weber's "harem messengers" delivering invitations to a Weber Royal Theater Party.

AN INVITATION

FROM THE EMPEROR
FOR TWO

"A FUNNY THING HAPPENED
ON THE WAY TO THE FORUM"
AT THE SHUBERT THEATRE
OCTOBER TWENTIETH — EIGHT P. M.
AFTER THE THEATRE,
CHAMPAGNE BUFFET WITH THE CAST
IN THE EMPIRE ROOM — PALMER HOUSE

WLS

EMPEROR WEBER

will be your host for the Theatre Party
on October 20, 1964
Tickets for the performance of
"A FUNNY THING HAPPENED ON THE WAY TO THE FORUM"
and admission medallions for the
Champagne Buffet after the Theatre are enclosed

WLS

Paul Revere and the Raiders.

£ 1,000

WEBE

W

Emperor Weber's
so-called "coin of the realm."

His Imperialness

★ 1 1 2 3 8 9 0 0 0 D

1 G

ONE

Chapter 8
Larry Lujack and WLS

In 1966, Dex Card decided to expand his outside business ventures and leave WLS. He was replaced by Larry Lujack, who had been brought to Chicago by WCFL from Boston and given their overnight show. Within a few short months, Gene Taylor and WLS made him an offer to join our station and do the afternoon "Silver Dollar Survey Show." So, in essence, we "stole" him away from WCFL. However, five years later, WCFL returned the favor and got Larry back.

Lujack's reputation both on and off the air was controversial. He had been fired by several radio stations over the years, was reputed to be cranky, as well as sometimes being moody both on and off the air. Larry had even supposedly insulted a sponsor on the air, resulting in a threatened lawsuit. He was described by some of his colleagues as looking like an "unmade bed," but those were the very traits that the teen audiences during the Vietnam War era of the late 1960s were attracted to. Remember, it was a time of rebellion, cynicism, and anti-authority, and those characteristics seemed to perfectly match Lujack's on-air persona.

At a staff meeting a week after Lujack was brought on board at WLS, the station's general manager, Ralph Beaudin, expressed his concern about the potential problems that we faced with our new, so-called "loose cannon." As I best recall, Beaudin had made his concern known to Gene Taylor, even before Gene hired Larry. Taylor was told that if Lujack crossed the line and created problems, he would be gone. Ralph placed all that responsibility squarely on Gene's shoulders and it didn't take very long for the concern to come to fruition.

Sears had just signed a $250,000 radio commercial contract with WLS that called for both Larry and me to do live commercials for that sponsor. Fifty years later I am still a little bit fuzzy on exactly what Larry said, but I believe it had something to do with Larry as a kid growing up on a farm in Iowa and using the Sears catalog for toilet paper. Larry's particular way of telling the story only served to compound the problem, and when a Sears senior vice president heard Lujack's proposed use of their marketing tool, he called their advertising agency and ordered that the contract with WLS be cancelled. WLS Sales Manager Bob Alexander called me, I called Gene Taylor, and we immediately went into damage control.

The first step was for us to meet with both the ad agency and the Sears people, profusely apologize for Larry's behavior, and promise that it would never happen again. Next, we gave Sears numerous free commercials to try to retain them as a WLS client. The final objective was to try to prevent Beaudin from ever hearing about the episode because Gene knew that Lujack would immediately become history at the station if our general manager ever got wind of the event. As it turned out, Beaudin never learned of the incident.

There seemed to be a pattern of behavior that Larry regularly repeated. Once a month, as program director, I would call an announcers' meeting and bring in the staff to discuss the format, music, and promotional events that were about to take place. Along with the occasional individual sessions, this was sufficient to keep the station and our staff on the right track.

However, when Lujack joined WLS, he had a questionable impact on the other DJs because they couldn't quite figure him out or if he intended to fit in. Before Larry, the mood at the station had been one of "let's get the job done, have fun, and enjoy each others' air skills." That seemed to change when Larry was hired because he tended to be a loner. During staff meetings, as I recall, he would sit in the corner of the room, say very little, and demonstrate what I considered to be disdain for the very purpose of the meeting. His favorite stunt was to roll up a piece of paper and pretend it was a telescope that he would use to scan the ceiling of the conference room. I felt that it was his way of demonstrating to me and the rest of the staff that he was a rebel and that what I had to say was of secondary importance to him. I would call him on it, but he would continue to do it in order to try to "rattle my cage."

Many years later, in his own book, *Superjock*, Larry wrote about his moods and his moments of deep depression. The WLS staff certainly had been aware that something was wrong. We had heard that he was going through a difficult divorce at the time, and figured that was the problem, although none of us approached him to talk about it. Larry would arrive at the station about noon, sit at his desk, put his cowboy boots up, drink coffee, smoke cigarette after cigarette, talk to no one unless spoken to, and stare at the blank wall. He would say nothing to anyone, but, around 3:00 P.M., he would amble over to the studio and go on the air.

Although we had supposed that he was just staring at the wall, Larry was actually preparing his on-air material. To the best of my knowledge, Larry never went on the air unprepared. He often sounded as if his jokes and observations came out of the blue, but that was certainly not the case. Lujack, like singer James Brown, was one of the hardest working men in show business and worked diligently to sound loose and unscripted, but was actually far from unprepared. It was the main reason that Larry lasted as long as he did on radio. He worked at it and, for the most part, management left him alone to do his thing.

I used to think to myself that one day I might be presented with a unique chance to extract my own form of revenge on Larry for his behavior and detachment. Well, sure enough, a year later I had my sought for opportunity. It was February 1967 when I found the chance to pay him back. Both Larry and I were hired to do appearances in adjoining towns one Friday night that month: Larry in Charleston, Illinois; me in nearby Mattoon. Because I was flying my plane to the Mattoon appearance, I suggested that Larry ride along with me, have his people pick him up at the Mattoon Airport, and then return with me later that evening. Larry was not, and as far as I know is still not, a fan of flying.

I made certain to assure him that I was a long-time, very competent pilot. The airplane was a new twin-engine Piper Aztec, and, by then, I had a copilot. Larry hemmed and hawed, but he recognized that it certainly made sense to fly with me rather than drive, so away we went on what turned out to be an uneventful flight to Mattoon.

Shortly after midnight on that bitterly cold winter night, Larry and I returned from our record hops to the airport for the flight home. Before we boarded the plane, however, I reached into the baggage compartment and handed Larry and his assistant inflatable life jackets. I told them that because of the wintry weather in Chicago, we might be vectored out over Lake Michigan before landing and that the life jackets were required by the FAA. Larry grumbled, but put it on.

As we took off and climbed into the frigid sky, I leveled the plane off at 5,000 feet and then my "secret plan" began to go bad. I suddenly pulled back on the throttle of the Aztec's left engine, stomped on the right rudder, and the twin engine Piper swerved. At the same time, my copilot reached back and purposely struck Lujack in the chest with his fist to inflate Larry's life jacket. However, because of the bitter cold, the rubber in the life jacket was brittle, and instead of inflating, it exploded and sent shards of rubber flying through the cabin. As I recall the incident, Larry turned a deathly shade of white. I apologized to him and told him how the joke had gone badly awry. Believe me, he was not amused. But, I wasn't done with Old Lar. Arriving in the Chicago area, I began descending for our landing at Sky Harbor Airport in Northbrook. I turned on the cockpit overhead light, and reached into the glove compartment and pulled out the aircraft operations and flight manual.

As I began thumbing through it page after page, Lujack quickly leaned over my shoulder, and, in a very concerned voice, asked what was wrong. I said that nothing was really the matter, but that I was just trying to figure out how to land the damn plane. Larry started banging on my shoulder, and said, in a voice bordering on hysteria, "Weber, cut the crap and get me down!" Once we landed, the propellers had hardly stopped when Lujack bolted from the plane. While he never flew with me again, he did hire a plane and pilot from time to time to get to his Midwest appearances, but always in a white knuckle mode.

A young "Old Uncle Lar" Lujack.

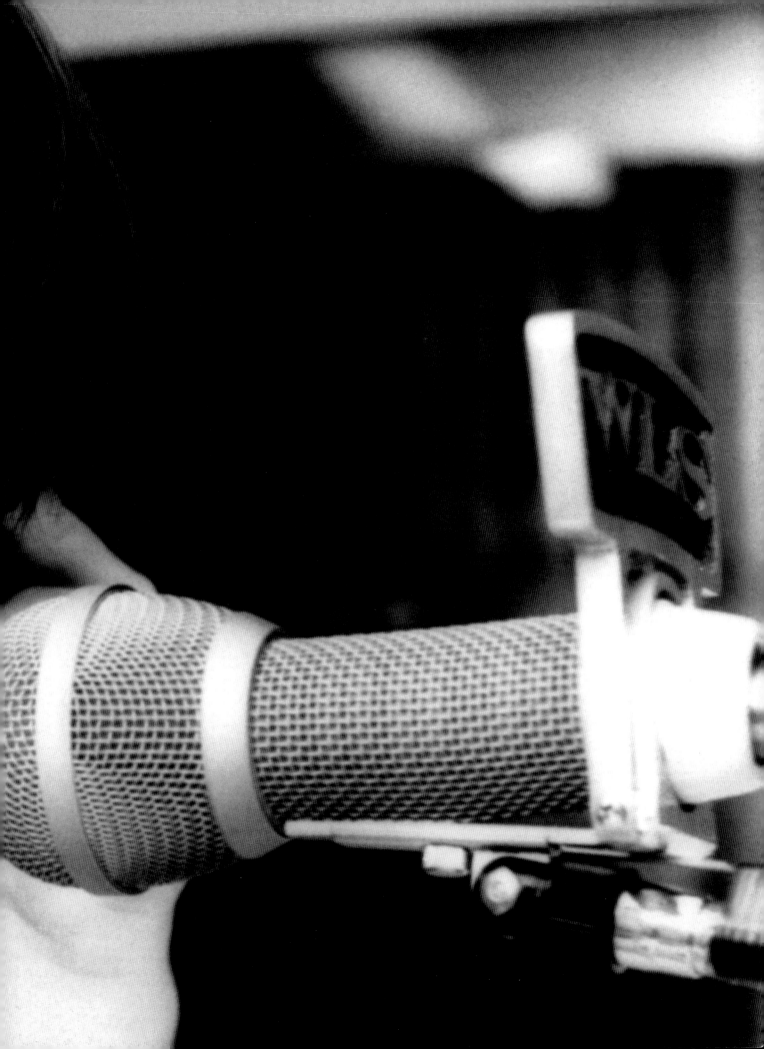

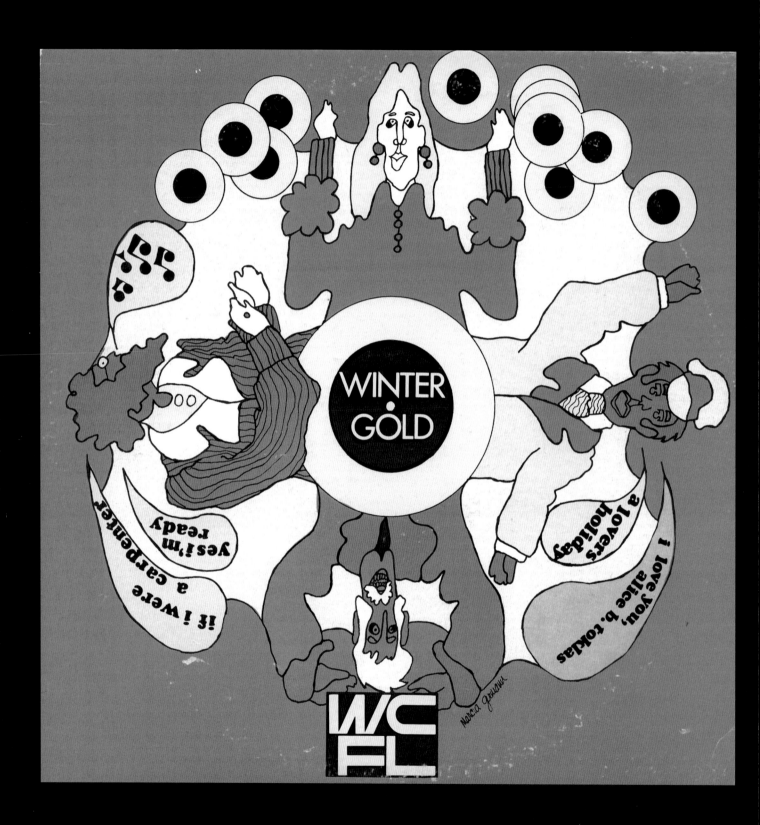

Chapter 9
WCFL and The Radio Wars

The Chicago Federation of Labor had created radio station WCFL in 1926 and indulged it like a spoiled child down through the years. They broadcast everything from soap operas to network shows as well as music covering the gamut from big band to jazz, but WCFL never was able to capture a sizable audience. However, the station was also not shy about spending money on good talent such as DJs Dan Sorkin, Sid McCoy, and Mike Rapchack.

By the mid '60s, the Chicago radio stations that had bit the bullet in the late '50s and early '60s by playing rock and roll were able to build large listening audiences, while many of the other Chicago AM stations experienced significant declines in their audiences and revenues. WLS just continued making a lot of money during those years as the premier rock and roll station in Chicago, and the station's ratings along with the profits were enormous. As a result, the Chicago Federation of Labor made the decision to get in on that action despite the fact that WLS had been rocking since 1960, was making money hand over fist for ABC, and had a six-year head start playing that genre of music. All those factors didn't seem to faze the Federation, and they decided to "play in the rock and roll marketplace." It all led to the Federation's decision to declare "war" against WLS. Of course, what helped WCFL was that the Federation was awash with union members' money, had tremendous clout in the city of Chicago, and figured they could put a stop to WLS' free rein on local radio.

The first action by WCFL was to hire program director Ken Draper from KYW in Cleveland and put him in charge of the station. Draper was a sharp, no-nonsense programmer with an eye and ear for rock and roll, and the Federation gave him a blank check to turn the station into a powerhouse. He literally brought most of KYW air staff with him to Chicago, including morning man Jim Runyon, Jimmy Stagg, and Dick Orkin with his alter ego, "Chickenman," as well as DJs Ron Brittain and Barney Pip. Draper even convinced his Cleveland office staff to join him in Chicago, and he made it very clear to them that this was "take-no-prisoners war." He even forbade his DJs to talk to WLS DJs if they met in a social situation. I think that Draper envisioned this as a crusade to attract listeners of rock and roll music.

As the drums of war sounded, WLS was very mindful of what was about to take place. I had only been the program director at WLS for little over a year, but was very concerned about the new challenge from 'CFL. At a meeting with General Manager Ralph Beaudin, I expressed my concern about the big trouble ahead. We began to lay out plans to counteract WCFL, including my proposal to increase our programming and production budgets, as well as several other areas, in order to heighten WLS' visibility.

Beaudin agreed to some of the increases and then leaned back in his chair and said to me, "They are going to give us a run for our money, but they are also going to run out of money!" This sounded nuts to me since the Federation of Labor had very deep pockets. In order to make his point, Beaudin asked me who was the first person to make a solo airplane flight across the Atlantic Ocean? It was an easy question, and I answered, "Charles Lindbergh!" Who was the second guy to do it? he asked. I had no idea, and Ralph responded, "It was an Australian guy named Bert Hinkler. He actually flew it in less time than Lindbergh and used less gas." I had never heard of Hinkler, I told Beaudin. "Exactly!" was Ralph's response. "In the public's mind, Lindbergh was first, and it doesn't matter who was second. In the listeners' minds, WLS was first with a rock and roll format by several years, and as long as we keep our focus, we'll continue to lead." Beaudin's advice certainly came true. However, it didn't happen before WCFL kept me awake at night worrying about our ratings and listening audience.

WCFL's promotions were short, clever, and they clearly appealed to the teenagers. First, there was the "Think Green" campaign in the spring of 1967 which involved the distribution of green, Styrofoam balls each with the 'CFL logo which listeners attached to their car antennas. People were awarded cash for exhibiting them. Then, there was a promotion that asked listeners to answer their phones by stating "Think Green With

left to right
**Art Roberts, Larry Lujack,
Chuck Buell, Jerry Kaye, Kris Erik
Stevens, and Clark Weber.**

"By the mid '60s, the Chicago radio stations that had bit the bullet in the late '50s and early '60s by playing rock and roll were able to build large listening audiences, while many of the other Chicago AM stations experienced significant declines in their audiences and revenues."

WCFL," and possibly be rewarded a couple thousand dollars. We even caught one of our WLS switchboard operators once answering our phone, "Think Green," in hopes she would win. While WCFL was able to move in and out of various promotions quickly, we were hobbled by the ABC corporate legal department back in New York. Everything had to be cleared with them, and it often took several weeks for the "legal eagles" to decide whether we should run various promotions. Finally, the "WLS Treasure Truck" took to the streets and a number of other WLS contests such as "Super Summer" flooded the airwaves.

WCFL's Dick Orkin was and is brilliant when it comes to catching the ear of the listener. "Chickenman," a take-off on Batman, was the story of a feathered crime fighter. He was priceless, and those episodes sound fresh 50 years later. As a result of Orkin and others at WCFL, within a few months, their ratings began to climb and reflect the station's efforts. It wasn't that they were creating new listeners, but rather that they were attracting listeners at our expense. Down through the years there were claims made about WCFL beating WLS in the ratings. In reality, although they were constantly within a few ratings points, they only beat us once during the summer of 1973. It was only a narrow victory for them, and probably just an anomaly since, in the fall 1973 rating book, WLS bounced back and WCFL never threatened again. However, no doubt, it was a great morale boost for the WCFL staff. But it was not something that the WCFL sales staff could easily sell because no ad agency would buy radio time based on one rating book—particularly a summer rating.

Radio stations live and die by the ratings as well as the need to have both national and local sponsors to provide ongoing income. The hypothetical "Bob and Betty Beercans Baby Boutique" and many other possible local sponsors can't keep a huge radio station afloat with just local sales revenue. The station must have the big bucks from national sponsors like automobile, airline, soft drink, and food companies in order to meet payroll and pay dividends to investors. Those national sponsors hire advertising agencies to determine, based on ratings, which stations have the largest target audience. The agencies then figure out the cost per dollar of reaching such listeners and make their ad buys accordingly. In almost all of the cases, national advertising dollars consistently were spent at WLS.

The evening DJs, at both stations, were focused on the teenagers who were in their listening audiences. Those kids constituted the biggest audience for rock and roll, and all of the WLS DJs worried about whether they would continue to listen to us during the other parts of the day. WLS had Ron Riley and Art Roberts in the evenings, while WCFL had the very talented Ron Brittain and an off-the-wall guy named Barney Pip. Pip and his trumpet, along with the command from him to "turn into peanut butter," helped him grow his audience. Pip's wife, whom we were never quite certain whether she was real or imaginary, supposedly would prowl the halls of the radio station at Marina City at night, spying on her husband to see if he had any young ladies in attendance. According to the late Jim Stagg, one night Pip's wife waited in her car in the Marina City parking lot where WCFL was located with the motor running. As the story goes, when Pip emerged from the building, she hit the lights and the gas, crashing her Volkswagen into the revolving door and narrowly missing Pip and a young lady. Thanks to the power of the Federation of Labor, the story never made the papers, and tragically, Barney later died in a car fire.

Without a doubt, the funniest person at WCFL was a lady who was never on the air. Mary Sweeney was a large, Irish woman who was the station's promotions director. She was quick to laugh and combined it with a wicked sense of humor. She loved to dress up as

"Radio stations live and die by the ratings as well as the need to have both national and local sponsors to provide ongoing income...The station must have the big bucks from national sponsors like automobile, airline, soft drink, and food companies in order to meet payroll and pay dividends to investors."

Clark Weber having a "bad hair day" while at WCFL.

a nun, and with her full figure she could pull it off. I was with her one day when she stopped at Marshall Field's in her nun's costume. We were on a packed elevator when she announced, "Oh, my God, my water just broke!" As we reached the ground floor with a stunned elevator full of people, she said to me, "Call Father Mike and tell him to meet me at the hospital. We're going to have a baby!" You can just imagine the consternation of the people on the elevator!

Another time, dressed in her nun's costume while aboard a TWA flight to Los Angeles, she was sitting in her seat when the plane's captain came walking down the aisle. Mary motioned to him to come over and then he said to her, "Yes, Sister. May I help you?" Sweeney whispered with an angelic smile, "Captain, when we get to L.A., I would like to throw such a jump into you!" The captain was so startled that as he stood up he banged his head on the overhead compartment, turned ashen white, and almost ran back to the cockpit. Sadly, Mary died several years later but not before she made a lot of people laugh at both her and themselves.

ALL HIT MUSIC

BIG 10

WCFL

COLLECTOR'S ISSUE NO. 6

The ONLY way to start a day: Corn Flakes, Coffee, and CLARK . . . your BIG TEN BREAKFAST . . . 6-10 daily!

Chapter 10
The Bat Phone and A Radio Divorce

In 1968, ABC announced they were promoting a guy from one of their smaller ABC stations to become WLS program director. I was elated since, for over a year, I had been asking to be relieved of the job. It was simply more than I could handle because it required me to get up at 2:30 A.M. to do the 6 to 10 A.M. morning show, make appearances across a four-state area, and do freelance voice work, all in addition to fulfilling the role of station program director. It was also negatively affecting my family life because I wasn't able to be home much of the time.

I had known the incoming program director for a while and had talked to him several times about the music we played. In fact, I found him quite knowledgeable about programming, and the word in the record industry was that he was quite competent. The only negative comments I had heard was that he might suffer from an over inflated ego.

What I didn't know was that the new program director was being sent to Chicago by an ABC executive in New York who I was told had "blood in his eye." According to 84-year old Mary Jane Johnson, at the time the executive secretary for General Manager Ralph Beaudin and Station Manager Gene Taylor, I learned that the New York executive had been passed over when Beaudin was made president of the ABC-owned and operated stations and might be seeking to have some sort of revenge. To compound the VIP's anger, Gene Taylor, had been made station manager over the executive's objection, and, supposedly, Gene expressed opposition to bringing in the new program director. That set the stage for what threatened to become a personnel "bloodbath."

It wasn't more than a week or two later when WLS Sales Manager Bob Alexander didn't seem to pay the proper respect to the new program director. It all started over some suggested log changes that the new PD had requested. When the program director was told to mind his own business, supposedly he went back to his office, called the VIP in New York, and said, in effect, "These boys won't play by my rules!" The VIP picked up his phone, called Alexander, and promptly fired him. What followed was the most divisive and contentious time in my 50-year broadcasting career.

In show business, we all expect changes and just adjust to them. WLS was certainly due to be tightened up and guided to new heights, but, to me, given the past direction of the station, the coming changes were a bit too rough to take. DJs Bernie Allen, Ron Riley, and our all-night disc jockey, Jerry Kaye, were all fired, and eventually, the talented Production Director Ray Van Steen was let go. I mean, really, who fires a very competent all-night man? According to retired engineer Dale Schimp, the new PD was on a roll and even tried to get Chief Engineer Roy Huberty fired, but Gene Taylor put his foot down and prevented it. And, with all the "blood on the floor," both Larry Lujack and I figured that we might be next. However, Mary Jane Johnson tried to assure us that we were protected, although neither of us felt in any way convinced that our jobs at the station were secure.

During this turmoil, two new voices were added to the station's on-air mix: Chuck Buell and Kris Erik Stevens. Kris was a mere 20 years old when he joined WLS, and while both Lujack and I thought he was a bit young and perhaps "green," Kris posted great nighttime ratings and remained with the station for three years. Then he eventually found his real calling as a Hollywood voiceover talent. Chuck joined WLS from Denver in 1969, but left in 1974 for San Francisco, later becoming the morning man for eight years on an oldies station in San Diego.

There are two ways a program director can provide leadership to his on-air staff. One is face to face and the other is in your face. Sadly, the new PD decided to use the latter approach, which involved introducing a gimmick used by several non-major market stations called the "Bat Phone." I knew about the technique and considered it strictly "bush league." It involved installing a phone in the studio next to the DJ's microphone. Instead of ringing, the phone had a red light on it so that when the program director heard something he didn't like, such as a record intro, DJ patter, or inappropriate segues, he would dial the "Bat Phone," the red light would flash, and the program director would often chew out the DJ

"In show business, we all expect changes and just adjust to them. WLS was certainly due to be tightened up and guided to new heights, but, to me, given the past direction of the station, the coming changes were a bit too rough to take. There are two ways a program director can provide leadership to his on-air staff. One is face-to-face and the other is in your face."

while he was on the air. I considered the whole technique juvenile and demoralizing, and while it gave the PD the power and clout he apparently felt he needed, it "ripped out the heart" of the DJ's on-air personality. When I listen to "air checks" some 38 years later, I can still hear the joyless delivery of the on-air staff after receiving one or several of those calls during a show. It's like a recent bumper sticker I saw that read, "The beatings will continue until the morale improves!"

The rancor between General Manager Gene Taylor and the program director seemed to heat up on a daily basis. Gene was a classy, well-mannered guy who was liked and admired by the WLS staff. He ran a tight but fair ship. However, it was quite apparent that he just couldn't accept the management style of the New York-appointed program director.
 One of the strangest changes the new PD made was to change the name of the "Silver Dollar Survey" to the "Music Radio Survey." To this day I'm asked to autograph "Silver Dollar Surveys," but I almost never see any copies of the "Music Radio Survey."

Two factors were working in the PD's favor. WCFL was beginning to lose some of its newfound popularity and the format at WLS was being tightened. New jingles were brought on board that highlighted "The Big 89" and the music rotation, or the number of times you heard a Top Ten tune went up considerably. Predictably, the ratings at WLS began to climb back up, although the station's claim of playing more music was somewhat bogus since it really involved more of the same most popular songs being rotated each hour. This results in more listeners, and that tends to drive up a station's ratings.

My morning ratings on WLS during the 6 to 10:00 A.M. shift were in good shape, and according to former WLS salesman Ed Doody, the station had spent $30,000 on a promotional five minute sales movie about my show. Nonetheless, the word in the industry was that I should watch my back. So, after working in what I considered to be a difficult environment for well over a year, I decided I had enough and no longer wanted to deal with the program director's management style.

Apparently, the word was spreading around the country that I was open to offers and several stations started sniffing around and making job proposals to me. WNBC in New York, KMOX in St. Louis, and KNBR in San Francisco were among the first. The KMOX general manager was supposedly cut from the same cloth as the WLS program director, and I certainly didn't want to go from "the frying pan into the fire." After weighing several offers, I decided to remain in Chicago and did so as a morning DJ and later as a morning talk show host for the next 26 years. The new WLS program director—the one responsible for creating the furor at the station—lasted just a short time and then suddenly parted company with ABC. His replacement, Mike McCormick, was ordered by the same New York VP, who had also hired the previous PD, to remove all the vestiges of the previous program director, including Art Roberts, Chuck Buell, and Kris Eric Stevens.

Meanwhile, WCFL management decided that perhaps one way in which they could beat WLS in the ratings was to hire some of the WLS on-air staff. After all, the thinking went, we were the people racking up the big rating numbers and if they could hire us then our audiences would naturally follow us over to WCFL.

In late 1969, WCFL offered me more money than I was making at WLS, along with a two-year contract, to do the morning show. At that time, I had a standard 13-week contract with WLS along with a program director who was probably going to march me out the door in the same way as the other DJs. I confess that as I typed my letter of resignation to

"Apparently, the word was spreading around the country that I was open to offers and several stations started sniffing around and making job proposals to me. WNBC in New York, KMOX in St. Louis, and KNBR in San Francisco were among the first."

"After I left WLS, the ABC corporate executives in New York were bound and determined to continue their "Ready, Fire, Aim" style of management during the early '70s."

Gene Taylor, I had tears in my eyes. For over eight and one-half years I had been a part of the most dynamic and influential radio station in America. I knew that I would never again be able to match the excitement that WLS had generated.

As I waited in the halls of WLS to see Gene and submit my resignation letter, his secretary, Mary Jane Johnson, asked me to reconsider my decision. When I recently interviewed Mary Jane for this book, she once again reminded me about that day and her request for me not to resign.

Looking back, I suppose that I could have survived and outlasted the program director, but to him, I know I represented another era and another style of handling both the programming and the staff. Plus, I was 39 years old and for a rock and roller DJ, that was getting a "little long in the tooth." On my last day at the station, after I cleaned out my desk and walked out of WLS, I stopped, and with a large lump in my throat, turned around for one last look. I realized how incredibly lucky I had been because not only was I a part of that outstanding radio station, I was a part of so many of my listeners' lives. There isn't a month that goes by now, 47 years later, that I don't run into someone whose life was touched by WLS. But it was time to move on.

After I left WLS, the ABC corporate executives in New York were bound and determined to continue their "Ready, Fire, Aim" style of management during the early '70s. Both the new WLS general manager and program director ruled with a "take no prisoners, shut up, and play the music" mentality. Larry Lujack was long gone, having been wooed back by WCFL for more money. WLS brought in a new lineup of very talented DJs, including Joel Sebastian, Gary Gears, J.J. Jeffrey, Bill Bailey, Bob Sirott, John Records Landecker, Yvonne Daniels, and Jeff Davis. According to Fred Winston, the new morning man, life at the station at that time was anything but pleasant. Fred, a very funny guy with a wicked sense of humor got into the same kind of trouble that Larry Lujack had gotten into a few years earlier; adlibbing a commercial and then getting carried away with it. The sponsor was the Yankee Doodle Restaurant chain in Chicago. Fred was raving about their food and went one step too far in his praise! He said, "the food is so good that it will yank your doodle dandy!" Newsman Lyle Dean completely lost it and when Fred realized what he had said, he lost it! The place was up for grabs and when Yankee Doodle heard about it, WLS lost it. The account that is! The station's ratings fell as WCFL won its one and only first place rating, and, by 1973, Program Director Mike McCormick was gone and Tommy Edwards had been brought in from WOR-FM in New York as the new program director. Although he had established an excellent track record, Edwards soon discovered what I had learned in the late '60s when I had been program director: you can't be on the air for four hours a day and then devote the rest of the day as program director since you are spread too thin trying to do both jobs.

In January 1974, John Gehron was hired from WCBS in New York to become the new WLS program director. It was just what was needed, and for the next 13 years, John guided the station through periods of ups and downs, but mostly ups. Tommy Edwards remained on his midday radio shift, and as production director, while John set out the steer the WLS "ship" out of troubled waters. He did so with a lot of class. Thanks to Gehron, the on-air staff remained mostly in place and there were no more firings, morale problems, or blood on the studio floor. Instead, he got the most from the station's talented staff and gave them the appropriate direction. What he did need to replace was the radio equipment, which Gehron said was so bad that when he arrived at WLS he was convinced that the equipment at his old, former college radio station was in better shape. It seems that ABC was taking its profits from the station and plowing it into their FM stations, and had made the decision to write off AM music radio as a lost cause.

Chapter 11
On To Marina City

When I stepped off the elevator in Marina City and walked into WCFL for the first time, I was met by a lot of familiar faces: Dick Biondi, Ron Riley, and Joel Sebastian, who had worked at WLS and had now taken root at WCFL. Combined with Jimmy P. Stagg, the off-the-wall antics of Ron Britain, and the teenaged "Pied Piper" Barney Pip, it made for interesting radio. Lew Witz, the station's general manager, and his staff welcomed me with open arms, and that was a delightful change from the acrimony I had left behind at WLS.

The format at WCFL was very similar to WLS, and the only basic difference was the lack of commercials. At WLS, I sometimes struggled to get all the commercials played, but that was not the case at WCFL. My new station may have been making money, but not much!

The radio war between WCFL and WLS was waged 24/7 with no holds barred for several years, beginning in 1965. However, it unraveled rapidly three short years later in 1968 when, according to Karen Draper, Ken's former wife, a clash took place between Draper as program director and the president of both WCFL and the Chicago Federation of Labor, Bill Lee. Draper announced that he wanted to beef up the WCFL news department and put reporters on the street to give his listeners a real look at what was happening in their city. They would report on crime, corruption, and cronyism in City Hall.

Bill Lee must have blanched at the very idea since the Federation was tight with Mayor Richard J. Daley and vice versa. The unions were one of the cornerstones of political power in Chicago with the ability to get out the vote for the mayor. In turn, the Daley administration supported the labor unions and helped give the Federation its power, and to put that in jeopardy was out of the question. Draper was equally adamant about creating a world class newsroom, and to add muscle to Draper's request, he said that if he didn't get the requested news staff he would walk away from the job. Lee said, no dice, thinking he would call Draper's bluff. In fact, Draper did indeed quit that very day, left Chicago, and went to California. From that moment on, the power and the momentum of WCFL began to decline, along with the morale of the air staff. After all, most of these people had followed Draper from Cleveland and their leader had left them in a lurch. The Federation moved quickly to fill the void by selecting Lew Witz, the sales manager, to fill Draper's job.

When I began working at 'CFL, I was given a freer hand on my show and immediately launched one of my goofier stunts. Women's liberation was becoming very popular around the country and, to do my part, I asked my female listeners to shed what some had come to consider as an anachronism of the times: their brassieres. I announced a WCFL "Ban the Bra" day and asked the women of Chicago to visit Marina City and drop off their bras. Notice that I didn't say "take off" their bras. The event was scheduled for noon on that summer day, and by 11:00 A.M. we began to realize that the promotion might cause us some trouble. Young men with high testosterone levels were gathering by the hundreds around Marina City, and the growing crowd was overflowing into our parking lot hoping to get a look at ladies who they assumed would be disrobing and shedding their bras. Officers of the Chicago Police Department were on hand to make certain that, indeed, there wasn't going to be any indecent exposure. The Chicago Federation of Labor was very nervous about the stunt, and as I stepped up to the microphone to welcome the cheering crowd, I'm sure it didn't help to defuse the situation when I told the crowd of mostly men to relax because "once you've seen one breast, you've seen them both!" The guys roared back, "We'll settle for one!"

A few brave, but nervous, women came forward and dropped off their spare bras in the container we had provided, all to the applause and thunderous approval of the men in the audience. When we had first planned the event, I suggested we hire a female impersonator to actually take off "his" bra and the crowd would discover it had been fooled. The station went ballistic and said my idea would cause a riot and just nixed the concept. I also suggested hiring a stripper who certainly wouldn't mind showing off "her charms." That idea also fell on deaf ears! The next day, the *Chicago Tribune* ran a tongue-in-cheek story complete with pictures that announced, "Ban the Bra is a Bust!"

"I would like to say that my arrival at WCFL caused the ratings to "go through the roof and over the wall into Waveland Avenue." But, it didn't quite happen that way. Yes, there were some increases in the show's ratings, but nothing to get excited about.

left to right
**WCFL Newsman,
Stan Dale with his pipe,
Clark Weber, and WCFL
secretary, Mary Silvestri.**

WCFL DJ Connie Szerszen

WCFL's
Clark Weber
Presents...
"FRIDAY
FALL-OUT"
DEPOSIT YOUR BRA HERE
FRIDAY, SEPT. 5 TH
12:00 NOON

"In the case of rock and roll, WLS had a four-year head start as the king of rock and roll in Chicago. So, being first is more important than being a late comer, and no amount of advertising will change that in the mind of the consumer."

Despite our stunt, the Chicago Federation of Labor was very sensitive about its reputation and went out of its way to maintain a squeaky clean image. Imagine the horror at the Federation when the station booked the Rolling Stones to appear at McCormick Place in 1970, and the group allegedly ran afoul of the law. I was the emcee of the show and knew something was up when the Stones arrived at the entrance to McCormick Place in Chicago Police squad cars. Immediately after their show, the group was hustled back into the squad cars and driven directly to O'Hare Airport. The Federation management was very upset, and according to the story I heard, the Stones were allegedly involved with an underage girl at their hotel. The power of the Chicago Federation of Labor held sway, and a story about that incident never appeared in the newspapers.

WCFL had both an ear for talent and an eye for beauty. I couldn't help notice the number of drop dead beautiful ladies employed by the station, from Bill Lee's secretary, Mary, to the switchboard operators. They all turned men's heads! I've always said that it doesn't cost any more to hire good looking women.

While I was working at the station, my freelance voice work continued to grow and that brought about a change in my appearance. When I auditioned for a national tire company's television commercial, the client said they didn't want a bald man selling their tires. I asked if I would be hired if I had hair on the top of my head, and when the answer was "yes," I immediately went out and bought a hair piece and was hired for the TV spot.

It's a strange thing about men in show business and their hair pieces. You see a lot of guys wearing them, and some are of good quality and expensive, while others are so bad they literally shriek at you. I used to tell Wally Phillips of WGN that he had a bad toupee. It wasn't that the piece was cheap, but that Wally didn't have any side hair to support the look of a full head of hair. Art Roberts of WLS had a good one, as did singer Steve Lawrence.

I didn't think much of Frank Sinatra's hairpiece, and the late columnist, Mike Royko, seemed to agree with me. He once wrote a story about Sinatra's hairpiece that ruined a party I attended. When Sinatra left Capitol Records to create his own label, which incidentally raised a lot of eyebrows, it was big news in music circles. I mean, how does a big star simply walk into a record company with whom he has been for years and not only announce he is leaving but also taking with him Dean Martin, Sammy Davis, Jr., and Trini Lopez? To celebrate their new record home, Sinatra and company decided to throw a party in Chicago at the Ambassador West Hotel.

Meanwhile, that day, Royko wrote his article about Sinatra's "ratty looking dome doily." When Joan and I arrived at the party, we were greeted by Dean and Sammy who welcomed us, and then began an apology. It seems that Royko's article had been pointed out to the volatile Mr. Sinatra, and he had responded very negatively. It was also about the same time that he was having conflicts with his girlfriend, Ava Gardner, and that may have added to his foul attitude. Although he was at the party, he stayed in a corner of the room by himself and was in no mood to talk to anybody. Frank made it quite clear that he wanted to be alone by surrounding himself with a couple of his burly bodyguards. To put it mildly, the party was less than a success.

I would like to say that my arrival at WCFL caused the ratings to "go through the roof, and over the wall onto Waveland Avenue." But, it didn't quite happen that way. Yes, there were some increases in the show's ratings, but nothing to get excited about. I worked diligently on my morning show and also began to do some market research on cause and

Clark Weber holding a "falsie."

The huge crowd outside Marina City waiting for the bras to fall.

effect that continues to this day. The information I gathered continues to help me in my advertising agency marketing today. What I discovered was that consumer perception is all-important in advertising since what the consumer believes is far more important than what we tell them. The company that is first to present the product has the best chance to win.

In the case of rock and roll, WLS had a four-year head start as the king of rock and roll in Chicago. So, being first is more important than being a late comer, and no amount of advertising will change that in the mind of the consumer. Is Hertz better than Avis? Maybe, but in the mind of the customer, Hertz was first and, therefore, had to be better. Can a company screw up its leadership and lose status? Absolutely, but WLS wasn't about to let that happen, even though it actually did so for a brief period of months in 1972 and 1973.

On the positive side, there were many great new people who joined WCFL when I was there, and just a couple of guys, Larry O'Brian and Bob Dearborn, come to mind. Dearborn was a classy and erudite DJ who was both funny and bright, with a good grasp of good radio. He continued to be successful in the radio business for years. Larry went to work at WTAE in Pittsburgh and held sway there for 20 years. After two years at 'CFL, when 1971 rolled around, I was pleased to end my contract with WCFL. They had treated me well, but, I was 41 years old and eager to explore the next chapter of my radio life.

While at the station, I had kept my nose to the grindstone and continued to strive for bigger ratings. However, it was like having been married to a beautiful movie star. When you're with her, you bask in her glory; but when the marriage is over, you are toast. The same held true with the other WLS DJs who also moved over to WCFL. To a man, including Larry Lujack, sooner or later we all realized that our stardom was based on our having been DJs at WLS, and when we changed stations, we were just some other rock and roll voices, albeit good ones.

Two years later, when WCFL "died," Gehron and General Manager Marty Greenberg had dinner with Larry Lujack and made him an offer to return to WLS to become the DJ on their morning show. It also helped that according to Gehron, under Larry's WCFL contract, they were required to pay part of his salary for several years after he returned to the "Big 89!" When Larry returned to WLS, he teamed up with Tommy Edwards to create what they called "Animal Stories," and several other on-air adventures that were downright funny, and that helped them boost their ratings. Meanwhile, at WLS-FM, Steve Dahl, and his sidekick Garry Meier, were making themselves known to a growing audience. Gehron proposed that both of them move to the afternoon slot on WLS-AM. Dahl didn't want to make the change because he felt that it would hurt his ratings. A court fight ensued, but Dahl lost the case and was forced to broadcast on WLS-AM. In the long run, Steve was the winner since, once he was on AM radio and exposed to another audience, his ratings and popularity soared. It was about the same time that ABC corporate grew tired of the New York VIP who had created so many problems at WLS down through the years, and they gave him the old heave ho. That is what I consider a delicious bit of irony!

There has always been a great deal of talk about the ratings battle between WCFL and WLS in the 1960s. There is no question that WLS was bruised by WCFL, but let's set the record straight. By July 1968, WCFL had been rocking for two years, was going full throttle, and, in the radio ratings at that time, received an 8.8 share of the total Chicago listening audience while WIND had a 12.3 share and WLS had a 14.9 share. One year later, in 1969, the "Pulse Radio Ratings" rating showed WLS with a 16 share, WCFL with an 11.5 share, and WIND fading with a 7 share. The WIND morning man, Howard Miller, had left the station about that time and most of his audience began to migrate to WGN.

It is true that WCFL did beat WLS in one rating book in 1973. However, when the next rating book came out, WLS was once again in the driver's seat. To have beaten the mighty WLS was a great morale boost for the 'CFL staff, but when they were unable to repeat the feat in the next rating book, it seemed to indicate that perhaps it was just a ratings anomaly. So, while WCFL, in the short run, certainly gave WLS competition, the bottom line is that 'CFL didn't make enough money. During the period when WCFL was on a ratings roll, the advertising economy, along with the nation's economy in general, had a major downturn. Apparently, the WCFL coffers weren't bringing in enough money to remain profitable. By 1976, WCFL's place in rock and roll history was just about over as they "turned off the lights, rolled over, and died." It had been a wonderful battle between two rock titans, and the audience benefited from the confrontation.

In later years I read that WLS even claimed to have beaten WGN in the ratings. While that may have been true, it was like comparing apples and oranges. WLS had huge 12 plus numbers, which referred to listeners who were ages 12 and older. WGN had prevailed with the so-called "money numbers," which included listeners who were ages 25 through 54, and, as a result, was and still is one of the top billing radio stations in the country.

A part of the story about my WCFL tenure is difficult to write simply because I was getting bored with rock and roll. I know that sounds like heresy, but it was the truth. The music had changed from joyful sounds and boundless fun during the '50s and '60s, to drug-related protests and voices of discontent in the '70s. A new generation of recording talent was beginning to be heard, and their musical voices were becoming more strident and crude. Radio was also just beginning to develop a hard edge to match the listeners' tastes in rock music.

Nancy Sinatra and Clark Weber.

Chapter 12
Talk
Radio

My Uncle Hank, the farmer, used to tell me, "Never get into a pissing contest with a skunk. He's very good at it, and even if you tie, you lose!" That's exactly the conflict that AM radio became embroiled in with FM radio and eventually lost. FM radio began playing a wider variety of music, and their DJs were allowed to develop fun personalities, which was exactly the way that AM radio had started out 15 years earlier.

The teens found FM to be new, fresh, exciting, and more in tune with their lifestyles. AM radio fought back by shortening their playlist and airing many of the same top hits over and over again. However, the AM stations also had begun to muzzle their on-air personalities.

A good analogy is to imagine two stores selling the same product. One store merely lays out a limited amount of merchandise it knows the buyer likes, with little input from the sales staff, while the other store trains its staff to greet you, help you with a much wider selection, and thank you for shopping there. In reality, the second store provides you with a fun shopping experience. That is basically what radio listeners were discovering. As a result, by 1975, FM commanded one-third of the radio market, and, according to the FCC, by 1981, that number would rise to 71% of the market. Rock and roll radio on AM stations around the country was beginning to hemorrhage with listener losses, and, by 1985, AM rock and roll radio was dead in the water.

Despite those shifts, soon after I left WCFL, Lee Davis, the program director at WMAQ-670 AM, approached me about signing a contract at his station and becoming the DJ during the station's afternoon drive time. The station was reeling from a disastrous relationship with a national radio consultant who had taken WMAQ and changed it from being a flagship NBC station. They used to have a fairly large older audience, but that changed when it became a rock station and they lost their core audience and were left with almost no measurable amount of listeners. My overall feeling about so-called radio consultants, in general, is quite negative.

NBC management in New York couldn't quite figure out the direction they wished to take WMAQ, so they kept on making changes in music to be played as well as station formats. Howard Miller, whose success in Chicago radio had been legendary, was doing the morning show at WMAQ. He and I had known each other for years, and, one day at lunch in the NBC cafeteria, Howard gave me a tip that changed my radio life. It was November 24, 1973 and my name appeared in Kup's Column in the *Chicago Sun Times* under the birthday heading of that day. Howard said to me, "How come you are so glum? It's your birthday." I said, "Yes it is, and I was just thinking that I'm 43 years old and still a DJ. I want to do more than spin records!" Howard responded, "Let me tell you what the next trend in radio will be. It's called talk radio, and a station in Denver is experimenting with it."

I could have just forgotten his comment, but something told me to pursue it further. The next day, I called the Denver station and got an on-air check copy of their "Talk Telephone Format" that featured Alan Berg as the host. Berg was a highly controversial personality who hosted a talk-show program that was often filled with shouting and name-calling. However, Berg's program electrified his Denver listening audience, although it sadly filled some listeners with such rage that a man took a machine gun to the radio station one night, waited in the parking lot, and shot Berg to death. That was not my idea of talk radio, although Berg's show did give me an idea of how the format worked.

I decided to begin rehearsing talk radio on my own, and several months later when WMAQ announced they were going to change the station's format to country and western music, they asked me to join in that change. I said, "No thanks," but I decided to ask Lee Davis if in the remaining three months of my contract I could try "talk" on the station. He said, "Go ahead, you can't hurt anything!" At the end of the three months, WMAQ went country. My response was to go across the street to WIND and say to Allen Mitchell, that station's program director, "I'm a talk show host, and I would like bring my format to your station." Within a short time, I was doing the 9 P.M. to midnight Contact show on WIND and the ratings began to climb. Allen allowed me a free hand with that show, and it was fun to do.

Every Friday night, I created a mythical nightclub called the "Boom Boom Room" complete with the sound effects of a popular watering hole. It was still an open line night where people could talk about anything. We claimed that we were broadcasting from high atop the 56th floor of the Westinghouse Hotel at the corner of Clark and Dearborn. Those two streets don't intersect, and the Yellow Cab Company soon complained to WIND about people hearing the show, hailing a cab, and wanting to go to the "Boom Boom Room." So, we changed the location to the corner of "Walk and Don't Walk." We also served a special beer that I shamelessly stole from Reg Kordick at KDKA in Pittsburgh. It was called, "Old Forthingslosh Stale Pale Ale—the only beer in the world with the foam on the bottom." In other words, we played with the audience and their imagination and they loved it. The ratings went up, and Westinghouse not only noticed those increases in my numbers but also recognized that AM rock and roll music was dying out. It was time for a change, and in 1976, WIND became the first talk show radio station with 24-hour all-talk shows.

By the end of 1981, WIND's talk show ratings were tied with WLS as AM 890 continued to lose listeners. Neil Sabin, who later became the vice president and general manager for Wiegal Broadcasting's WCIU and WMNE in Chicago, was the producer of my talk show. Fellow talker, Dave Baum, who is still dollar-for-dollar one of the best talk hosts in town, along with Lee Rodgers, Joel Sebastian, Norman Mark, "Chicago Eddie Schwartz," and Steve King rounded out our talk staff.

In those early days of talk radio, we were on a seven-second tape delay. People think that it was used to prevent foul language, while it was really a tool for us to prevent lawsuits. Without the tape delay, we had no way of stopping lewd stories from going out on the air. By having the delay, we could hit the big red button at our elbow in the studio and a voice would say, "I'm sorry, but we have to cut away. This is WIND Chicago." When the listeners heard that, they figured that someone was either using profanity or saying something libelous. I remember one day when my guest was the famous Dr. Norman Vincent Peale, the noted theologian, author, and all-round nice guy whom I had interviewed several times through the years. As I introduced him to my radio audience, I reached over to shake his hand but accidentally hit the red button with my elbow. The audience heard, "I'm sorry, but we have to cut away. This is WIND Chicago." With that, the station's switchboard lit up with listeners wanting to know what profane or libelous statement Dr. Peale had uttered on the air. So, when we returned to our broadcast, I was quick to explain what had happened, and, to my delight, Dr. Peale was laughing so hard he was in tears.

A charming young lady named Johnny Putman joined our WIND air staff, and she mentioned to me that she had never flown in a small plane and asked me to take her up for a flight. I offered to fly her to Lake Lawn Lodge in Wisconsin for lunch so that she could discover the joys of flying. Suddenly, a very upset Steve King let me know that Johnny wasn't going anywhere with me since he wanted to marry her. I was surprised, and so, perhaps, was Johnny. It wasn't long after that they got married. At the reception, which Joan and I attended, Steve played guitar and serenaded his bride with a rendition of the old Chuck Berry classic, *Johnny Be Good.*

By 1981, several generations of teenagers had grown up claiming WLS-AM as their rock and roll home. While the on-air talent at the station was excellent and the revenue stream was still good, there are a few inescapable facts that need to be noted. FM radio in the '80s had a firm grip on a large segment of that audience and, not unlike TV, audiences had

The teens found FM to be new, fresh, exciting, and more in tune with their lifestyles. AM radio fought back by shortening their play list and airing many of the same top hits over and over again. However, the AM stations also had begun to muzzle their on-air personalities.

Top 56 Of '76

DAVE BAUM
5:30-10 am

CHUCK BENSON
10 am-2 pm

1. TONIGHT'S THE NIGHT/Rod Stewart
2. SILLY LOVE SONGS/Wings
3. BOHEMIAN RHAPSODY/Queen
4. DON'T GO BREAKING MY HEART/Elton John & Kiki Dee
5. DISCO DUCK/Rick Dees
6. DECEMBER, 1963/Four Seasons
7. AFTERNOON DELIGHT/Starland Vocal Band
8. CONVOY/C. W. McCall
9. LONELY NIGHT/Capt. & Tennille
10. IF YOU LEAVE ME NOW/Chicago
11. WELCOME BACK KOTTER/John Sebastian
12. SHOP AROUND/Capt. & Tennille
13. I WRITE THE SONGS/Barry Manilow
14. BOOGIE FEVER/Sylvers
15. PLAY THAT FUNKY MUSIC/Wild Cherry
16. I ONLY WANT TO BE WITH YOU/Bay City Rollers
17. SHANNON/Henry Gross
18. 50 WAYS TO LEAVE YOUR LOVER/Paul Simon
19. DISCO LADY/Johnnie Taylor
20. DEVIL WOMAN/Cliff Richard
21. GOT TO GET YOU INTO MY LIFE/Beatles
22. RIGHT BACK WHERE WE STARTED FROM/Maxine Nightingale
23. MUSKRAT LOVE/Capt. & Tennille
24. THEME FROM "S.W.A.T."/Rhythm Heritage
25. DREAM ON/Aerosmith
26. GET CLOSER/Seals & Crofts
27. ROCK AND ROLL MUSIC/Beach Boys
28. A FIFTH OF BEETHOVEN/Walter Murphy
29. GET UP AND BOOGIE/Silver Convention
30. YOU ARE THE WOMAN/Firefall
31. LET 'EM IN/Wings
32. I'D REALLY LOVE TO SEE YOU TONIGHT/Eng. Dan & John F. Coley
33. LOVE ROLLERCOASTER/Ohio Players
34. MORE THAN A FEELING/Boston
35. SATURDAY NIGHT/Bay City Rollers
36. LOVE HANGOVER/Diana Ross
37. HAPPY DAYS/Pratt & McClain
38. MORE, MORE, MORE/Andrea True Connection
39. SHAKE YOUR BOOTY/K.C. & the Sunshine Band
40. BREAKING UP IS HARD TO DO/Neil Sedaka
41. DREAM WEAVER/Gary Wright
42. WRECK OF THE EDMUND FITZGERALD/Gordon Lightfoot
43. ROCK'N ME/Steve Miller
44. LOVE TO LOVE YOU BABY/Donna Summer
45. LET HER IN/John Travolta
46. YOU'LL NEVER FIND ANOTHER LOVE LIKE MINE/Lou Rawls
47. THE BOYS ARE BACK IN TOWN/Thin Lizzy
48. LET YOUR LOVE FLOW/Bellamy Bros.
49. BETH/Kiss
50. YOU MAKE ME FEEL LIKE DANCING/Leo Sayer
51. YOU SHOULD BE DANCING/Bee Gees
52. NADIA'S THEME/Barry DeVorzon & Perry Botkin, Jr.
53. RUBBERBAND MAN/Spinners
54. FOX ON THE RUN/Sweet
55. ALL BY MYSELF/Eric Carmen
56. NEVER GONNA FALL IN LOVE AGAIN/Eric Carmen

STU COLLINS
2-6 pm

CONNIE SZERSZEN
6-10 pm

CLARK WEBER
"Contact" 10-Midnight

ED "Chicago" SCHWARTZ
Midnight-5:30 am

560 WIND RADIO
▲ First on your dial.

Lee Rodgers

Dave Baum

"In those early days of talk radio, we were on a seven-second tape delay. People think that it was used to prevent foul language, while it was really a tool for us to prevent lawsuits."

become bored with anything related to earlier generations. Like Norma Desmond, the silent movie star in the Broadway show, Sunset Boulevard, WLS was aging and the radio industry was slowly but surely moving ahead without her.

During the summer of 1984, WLS slipped to 16th place in the ratings. Many of us in radio held our breath hoping "the Great Lady" would regain her throne. It wasn't to happen. The station held on for three more years before the announcement was made that it was all over and that WLS would become a "news/talk" station. In its new role, the station once again became a powerhouse and continues to set standards in the broadcast arena.

Nonetheless, on August 28, 1987, Chicago's premier rock and roll station died. Larry Lujack bid farewell on the air on behalf of the air staff, and there wasn't a dry eye in the house. I had the same sad reaction while sitting in the front seat of my car just listening to the end of an era. It is estimated that during its 28 years of rocking, at least 60 DJs held claim to the fact that they were, at one time or another, an integral part of one of the most exclusive and powerful radio stations in America.

To those of you who have listened to me on the radio, and were transported back in time as a result of this book, thank you for your radio loyalty and just know that it was an honor to entertain you both then and now!

"On August 28, 1987, Chicago's premier rock and roll station (WLS-AM) died. Larry Lujack bid farewell on the air on behalf of the air staff, and there wasn't a dry eye in the house."

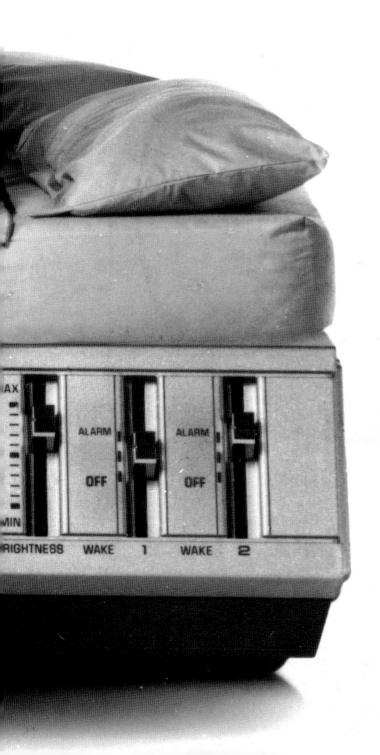

Index

And, finally, here is a thought
for the day:

I'd rather be a COULD BE
If I can't be an ARE;
Because a COULD-BE is a MAY-BE
Who might be reaching for a star.

I'd rather be a HAS-BEEN
Than a MIGHT-HAVE-BEEN by far,
For a MIGHT-HAVE-BEEN
 has never been
But a HAS was once an ARE.

*Mother Weber's
Oldest Son Clark*